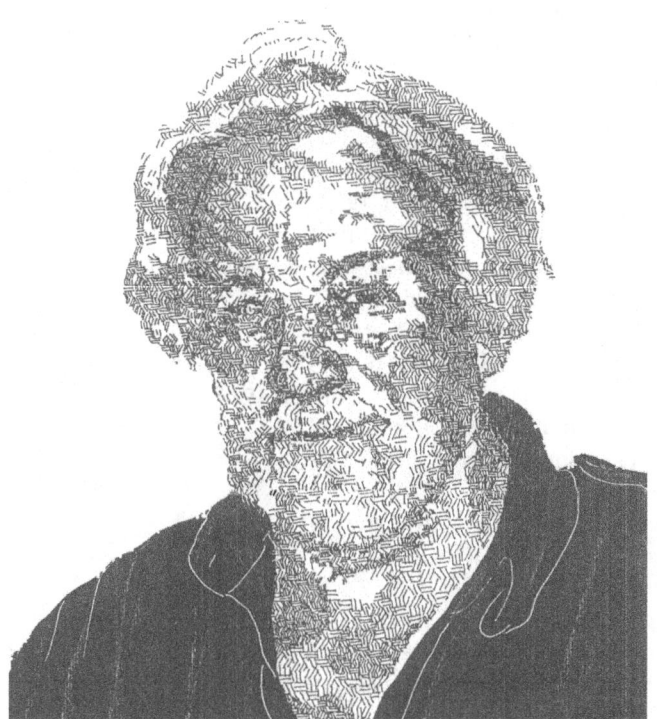

Colin Simms – poet, naturalist, and lifelong independent observer – was born in 1939, and lives as an author and freelance naturalist in the North of England, with journeys throughout the northern hemisphere, wherever his objectives live – his homes have been where the martens, otters, birds of prey and other enthusiasms are. He is not an orthodox conservationist, but insists on the privacy, 'isness', for wildlife which modern trends deny. He also demonstrates the poet-naturalist's concern for precise observation, apposite language and cadence. North American wildlife and the Native American tribes, and their history, have been a life-long fascination of his; this volume brings together all of his long poems, and a large number of shorter poems on these themes.

Colin Simms — selected bibliography

Lives of British Lizards, Goose and Sons, Norwich, 1970.
Some Effects of Yorkshire Flooding (with J. Radley), Sessions Book Trust, York, 1971).
Pomes and Other Fruit, Headland, Sheffield. 1972.
Adders and Other Worms, Headland, Sheffield, 1972.
Working Seams, North York Poetry, York, 1972.
Bear Skull, North York Poetry, York, 1972. (Revised edition, 1974)
Birches and Other Striplings, Headland, Sheffield. 1973.
Modesty (Swaledale Summer), Headland, Sheffield. 1973.
Pine Marten, Seven Prints, Genera 14, York, 1973.
Horcum and Other Gods, Headland, New Malden, 1975, 1976.
Jane in Spain, Genera, Newcastle-upon-Tyne, 1975.
Photosopsis for Basil Bunting, Headland, New Malden, 1975. (2nd edition, 1986.)
Rushmore Inhabitation, Blue Cloud Quarterly, Marvin, SD, 1976.
No North Western Passage, Writers' Forum, London, 1976.
Flat Earth, Aloes Books, London, 1976.
Parflèche. Galloping Dog Press, Swansea. 1976.
Otters: Ten Seals, Genera 16, Newcastle-upon-Tyne, 1976.
Voices, The Many Press, London, 1977.
Humility, Spanner, London, 1977.
On Osgodby Cliff, Curlew Press, Harrogate. 1977.
Windscale: Four Cantos, Genera Editions, Newcastle-upon-Tyne, 1978.
Midwinter Housewife, twisted wrist, Hebden Bridge, 1978.
Pentland, Shadowcat, Weardale, 1978.
Some Company (Tea at 40), Genera Editions, Newcastle-upon-Tyne, 1979.
Hunting Bunting, Luksha, New York & San Francisco, 1979.
Ingenuity (Wensleydale Winter), Shadowcat, Weardale, 1979.
Spirits, Shadowcat, Weardale, 1980.
Movement, Pig Press, Durham, 1980.
Time over Tyne: Poems, The Many Press, London, 1980.
A Celebration of the Stones in a Watercourse, Galloping Dog, Newcastle, 1981.
A Second Book of / Look at Birds, Genera Editions, New York, 1981. (2nd edition, 1989).
Cuddie Cantos, Bellingham, 1986/7. (2nd edition 2000.)
Eyes Own Ideas, Pig Press, Durham, 1987.
Luigi Pirandello: Navigator, Shadowcat, Weardale, 1988.
In Afghanistan: Poems 1986-1994, Writers' Forum, London, 1994. (2nd enlarged edition, 2001.)
Poems to Basil Bunting, Writers' Forum, London, 1994. (2nd enlarged edition, 2001.)
Shots at Otters, RWC, Reading, 1994.
Goshawk Lives, Form Books, London, 1995.
Bewcastle & Other Poems for Basil Bunting, Vertiz, USA, 1996.
Otters and Martens, Shearsman Books, Exeter, 2004.

The American Poems

Colin Simms

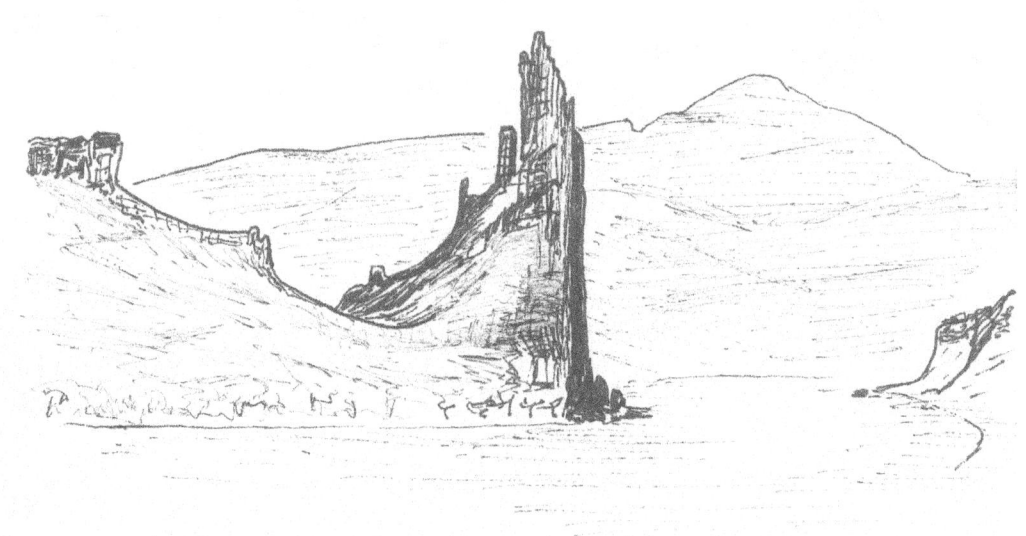

Shearsman Books

First published in the United Kingdom in 2005 by
Shearsman Books,
58 Velwell Road
EXETER EX4 4LD

www.shearsman.com

ISBN 989-0-907562-93-1

Copyright © Colin Simms, 1976, 1977, 1980, 1987, 2005.

The right of Colin Simms to be identified as the author of this work has been asserted by him in accordance with the Copyrights, Designs and Patents Act of 1988. All rights reserved. No part of this publication may be reproduced, stored in a retrieval system, transmitted in any form or by any means, electronic, mechanical, photocopying, recording or otherwise, without the prior permission of the publisher.

Acknowledgements:
The seven long poems included here first appeared as follows:
No North Western Passage (Writers' Forum, London, 1976)
Carcajou in *Eyes Own Ideas* (Pig Press, Durham, 1987)
Missouri River-Songs (Genera Editions, 1980)
A Celebration of the Stones in a Watercourse (Galloping Dog Press, Newcastle-upon-Tyne, 1981)
Parflèche (Galloping Dog Press, Swansea, 1977)
Rushmore Inhabitation (Blue Cloud Quarterly chapbook nº 2, Marvin, SD, 1976)
The Compression of the Bones of Crazy Horse (Poetry Review, Vol. 67: 1 & 2, 1977)

Some of the shorter poems printed here first appeared in the following: *Blue Cloud Quarterly, Limestone, London Review of Books, New Hope International, Planet Drum Review, Poetry North-East, Poetry Review, Quickenings, Spectacular Diseaes; SubVoicive Poetry, Adders & Other Worms* (Headland Poetry Publications, Sheffield, 1972); *Bear Skull* (2nd edition, North York Poetry, York, 1974); *The Other Poetry Book* (ed. G. Sargent, Northwoods Press, Bigfork, MN, 1974); *Black Hambledon – Black Hills Songs* (Genera Editions, Newcastle-upon-Tyne, 1977); *Voices* (The Many Press, London, 1977; *Some Company* (Genera, Newcastle, 1980); *A First Book of Birds* (Genera, Newcastle, 1980); *A Second Book of / Look at Birds* (Genera, New York, 1981); *Time Over Tyne* (The Many Press, London, 1981); *Eyes Own Ideas* (Pig Press, Durham, 1987). Some of these poems were also read on Radio KTCY; Radio Raleigh, NC; Radio KRAB. The author extends his thanks to the editors and publishers for their support.

The illustrations on the title page, on the section title for Missouri River Songs, and on page 58 are all by Colin Simms: respectively, 'Prairie Falcon Lookout, Upper Missouri'; 'Mountains beyond river and a high terrace of the Upper Missouri'; 'Cattlepath to summer pasture, Montana'. The cover shows a photograph by the author of a Ghost-Dance costume worn by one of his ancestors in the 1890s. The costume is made from mule-deerskin and the feathers of prairie-mountain meadow birds. All of these illustrations and photographs are copyright © Colin Simms, 2005. The portrait of Colin Simms on the flyleaf, and the 'Crazy Horse' woodblock on page 129 are by E M Makepeace and are reproduced here by permission of the artist. Copyright © E M Makepeace, 1995, 2005.

CONTENTS

Author's Note	7
No North-Western Passage	9
Carcajou	35
Missouri River Songs	47
A Celebration of the Stones in a Water-Course	59
Parflèche	89
Rushmore Inhabitation	111
The Compression of the Bones of Crazy Horse	129
Shorter Poems:	139
The Thieves' Road	141
Coming Off the Hills, Urra	142
Rocky Mountain Locust Strewn	143
April in 1622, High Plains	144
'Allied Extermination'	145
Crossing Minnesota, West	146
'Blue-blooded'	147
There is not difference, we are all offence	148
Gray Alders	149
Storm Crossing Texas	150
'Giving is everything', but only a hint	151
Bear Skull	152
Snake turns through the great trench of West Wyoming	153
Fasting, to the Arapaho Sundance	154
Thinking, Put in Mind of Kerouac	155
At Pine Ridge, 1973	156
Targs	157
Sami in their tipis	158
George Catlin artist from the early 1830's	159
'Medicine Deer' Rock	161
Equipment for Taxidermy	162
Clark's Nutcracker	163
Ptarmigan	164
Great Northern Diver (her Common Loon)	165

loon-call for all long shorelines . . .	166
Snowy Owl	167
MacKay's Snow Bunting	168
Riding: The Platte, Nebraska	169
Fire Place	170
Padding Words Stalk Some Passing Cat	171
Mount Rainier	172
Aplomado Falcon	173
from Black Hambledon – Black Hills Songs	
Black Hambledon	174
Sturgis	175
Topcliffe, Up the Escarpment	176
Bad River, Teton	177
We wanted to look at War Cloud's paintings	178
Short Stack with Navaho	179
Bobcat	180
NNWP	181
Beaver-Lodge reality	182
Being in the Bin, or the Irrelevance of 'Recycling'	183
High Rockies, October 1997	185
'American Marten, Replacing the Pine Marten in England'	186
G.T.T. 1984	187
from 'Climbing': Book 5 of 'Tea at 40'	188
Hell Canyon, on Snake River, Idaho 1973	189
The Pine Ridge Gyrfalcon	190
Prairie	191
The Book of Nature	192
New Airframe	193
from Tea at 40	194
Quake, Communicate	195
The Cypress Hills, and Barrens	196
Agelaius phoeniceus	197
Mississippi Floods at Moline, April 1973	198
Smelt	199
The Place You Recommend	200
New Drift Country . . .	201
Passenger Pigeon, Extinct 1914	202
Mass Movement	203
From an Unfinished 'American' Long-Poem	204

Author's Note

Acknowledgements must be attempted, and a few pointers to other realities. Readings given at a series of Quaker meetings and Methodist Missions gave many early contacts amongst The People. For encouragement at critical points in my involvements, 'politics' and 'poetry', many in North America and Britain and Eurasia are responsible and some I know don't want mentioning here. A few names are in the text. Many remembered with gratitude and a few who are mostly dead now: Sid Chaplin, Basil Bunting, Benét Tvedten, Chris Grieve ('Hugh MacDiarmid'), Marlon Brando, Bob Mitchum. Earlier publishers, especially Bob Cobbing, Peter Hodgkiss, Eric Mottram, Gary Greenup and John Welch were very supportive, as were a few journalists in Britain and America but not the *Sunday Times* who reneged on me at Wounded Knee II. Joy Ufford over thirty years, relatives of mine over there even longer, have made a lot of work possible, and for hospitality over thirty years' of visits, 1967-97, on reservations, in camps, in homes of all sorts – hogans, tepees, trailers, log and tar shacks, ranches, 'hotels' … Hospitality here in return to several, with whom I've walked and ridden the Scottish Borders and West, Cumberland and Northumberland and the Durham Dales and Yorkshire Dales and North Riding moors.

Amerindian music was and is essential; texts from Frances Densmore on 'Native American Ceremonial songs' tapes †7702A and B (1977) (Leonard and Mary and Christine Crow Dog), Jerome Rothenberg's 'Horse Songs' and "total translations" of Navaho songs originally sung by Frank Mitchell (7707A). These, and earlier versions, were transcribed and prepared from time to time by careful friends who have also proved critics in their different ways and persisted with me – including Mary Hider, Lesley Simms, Vivien Taylor, Bob Cobbing, Harry Gilonis, E. Kelly and Margaret Hartley. The Native Americans Paul War Cloud, Leonard Crow Dog, Gladys Bissonette are only a few of the many reservation and other men, women and children, from Manitoba to Arizona and Oklahoma, Alaska to Baja California and in cities – especially Seattle, St. Louis, San Francisco, Denver, Chicago, Los Angeles and New York – who helped, all sorts of ways, and provided good crack. Some of these pieces were written in their homes; as was 'NNWP' at Muirburn and Brownsbank‡ in Lanarkshire in the company of Chris Grieve and his wife Valda. My thanks to all. May my inadequacies spur on others…

Colin Simms, 2005.

† For instance: available also with Jackson Mac Low, Charlie Morrow and other poets on 7711 A (1977) from the New Wilderness Foundation, Inc., 365 West End Avenue, New York NY 10024.
‡ From a tape-recording of that meeting, following a reading of the poem:
    C.S.— "…and *that* is surely *too long*?"
    C.M.G.— "Oh, [laughing] – it is not *long enough*! Each of these American long-poems are remarkable … and powerful *enough*: ye ken ye hev a subject of muir importance than anything I've read for a long time. God!…"

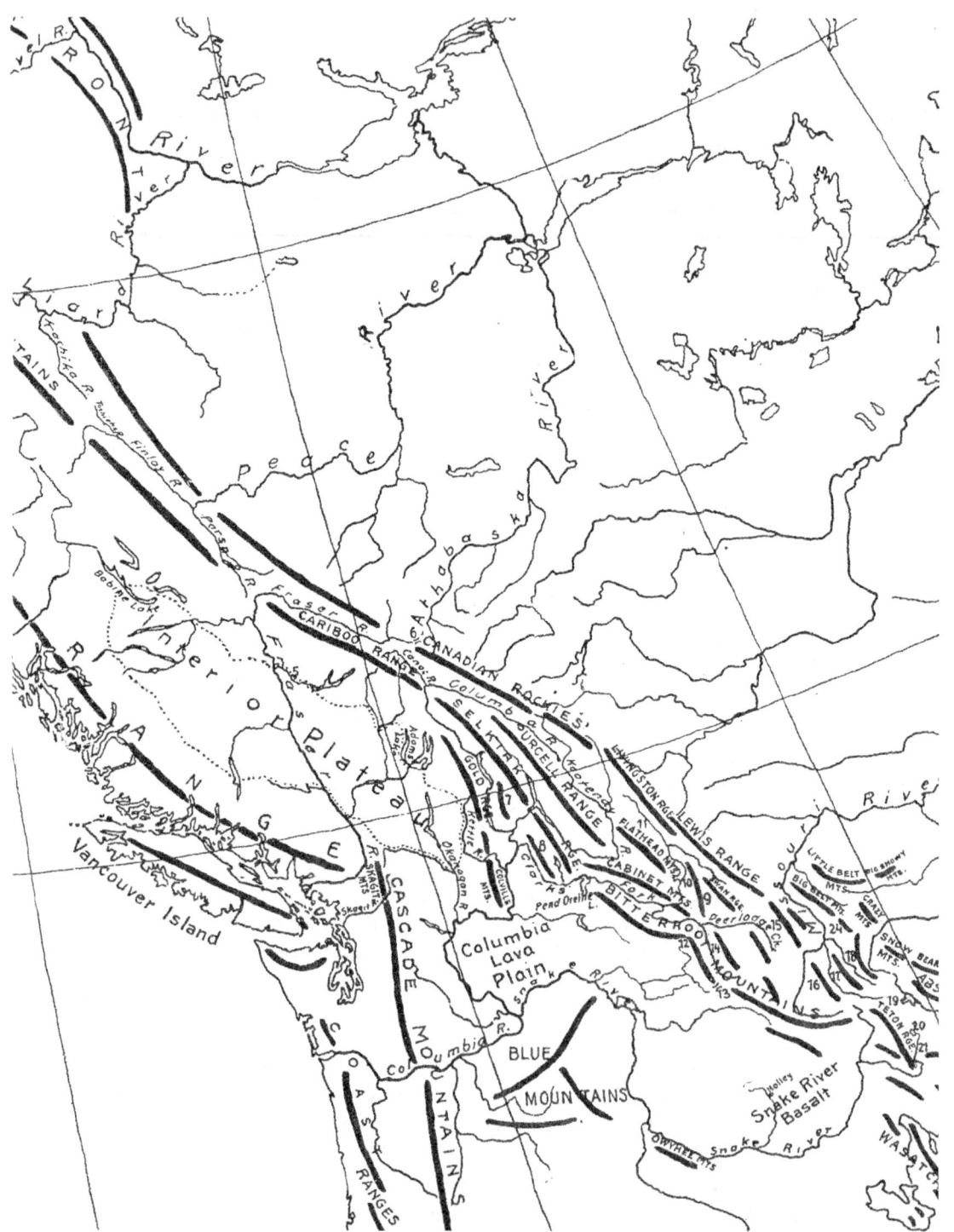

No North-Western Passage

a long-poem (three voices)
for R.R.

But my soul sent a woman, a woman of the wonderfolk,
A woman as fire upon the pinewoods crying 'Song, a song.'
As the flame crieth unto the sap
My song was ablaze with her and she went from me

—Ezra Pound, from *Personae*

Son of a border grieve, a boy in Yorkshire's Cleveland
what was it in his mind at Aireyholme Farm
why do we have to go so far for it   to go so far:
In a cloyed place where a first word might   be last
at Aireyholme, Cleveland, where James Cook cut corn
separating one man from his way   to chase   because he's seen
or thought he's seen enough : that one thing following on the wind worth waiting for.
Some *Voyageur* might have named it other, but Cook, put on the hook
after Santa Monica: where he'd been a few miles a-drift
and to call it   Cape Flattery : because 'it first bid us fair' but
(his *Resolution* logged) 'proved an inhospitable shoreline'.

I Cape Flattery (48° 38' N., 124° 73' E.)

As Rachel feared the white seal-cub in the rocks at Kettleness (54° 51' N., 0° 43'.)
The ripples cleared to show slow sea-otters in the kelp
                                grooming by hand and gentleness
needing constant assurance of one another, embracing when they're anxious
knocking and rocking together like swelled logs on rocks
                            'you're only interested to flatter me'
you object to my best poem for you that what I have to say is not quite true.
Whitby is a statement out of the mouth of the Esk and the sea.
                                     Poetry is the truth we got
          to see
whether it happened quite that way or not
                                  The Celts and Romans met at the Whitby Synod
in the seventh century
             so that sailships and otters can bear the same name
             the headlands enclose the Bay : whatever it is we see.
The *Rachel* made only one voyage out of Whitby
a whaler, 1776, on the Greenland Game
but there is no record of her foundering
nor of any change of name
             we're coming back round to thinking of this in Whitby.
Emily and Anne Bronte's cycle, the Gondals discovering Gaaldine, a dream
derived from Oliver Goldsmith's 'Grammer of General Geography'.
Gondal a large Island in the North Pacific (next to the entry for the unknown Gaaldine)
implied to be exotic   girls as quixotic as   about high land
                           eventually, they reached Vancouver Island
feeding on mere crabs, hind webs in the air to save heat loss,   poor otters
     at Nootka sound and were offered   (28th March 1778)
        'friendship, the flesh still on the hands and heads'
    we'd call them Trophies now
               only one or two of them nibbled. It was needed.
Living fur, type of the economy of nature, is the only luxury   see
    there isnt always time to check
                          images or instruments, we 'learn to have
    is to trust the quick view'   Cook of his sextant.
Like me to you   or the otters to both of us, who nearly took them to
                                              extinction
with demand for furs in the Depression   in our Ark   after all that, the old man needed
       reassurance, or Clerk   the small beer all extinguished

                would not have named the next Cape after Cook
       the least distinguished   headland of the entire voyage
who after getting Santa Monica all wrong from the stars
                                             was really on the hook
and making mistakes got to him (Cook)   not just in case they got into the book
   for our historical sources   *the stars must have moved their courses,*
I will remember Cape Flattery   my head-land
Space for my morning stride   Whitby Strand, you at my side
sky, heather, and sea   moved over for me   back in Whitby
where you looked away from the   the motel pattern banned patinas
                'NO INDIANS'   *They* say 'We were the richest people in art and myth
but in our dance we looked around us and the place was gone
if you look around you, you forget the steps within:
                                we offered Cook more than he could bring
              away.   And he went away'
                                That was a good day
                                                Northward to Nootka
and they went to cutting trees down for the new masts they saw
would be needful to enable them to make the Northwest Passage
and burst into the Atlantic from the Pacific
ate wild raspberries and junipers,
                            took down 150 foot conifers
'The centre of the world for us is this dances dancers are walking bears and flashing salmon'
'We are for you.   You went'
                  didnt find the Passage, the short cut home
and none of them then, but all of them since, were sure that they'd be back.
'They had our country! It had served us for
they had it but in no legal possession
                         what we had been discovering had been
what was in their minds who named it first.   It mattered.
                    'Cape Flattery' and before Cape Flattery
we called it New Albion   after Scotland where Cook's father was from: (Jacobite)
         it had the same spread of hills   'In trust   could not be trusted'
'we judged ourselves to be clear of danger
                          but soon found otherwise'
(Cook's log at Cape Flattery, and the sense   provoked
                delay, but the word he used was 'dally'
      as you might linger in   new land
 and we should leave on it
             not too many signs of our being there   when we go!

II Astoria

From the port that built the *Endeavour* and *Discovery* for them
deep-hulled colliers   two-storeyed
we came upon the place they had   looked forward to,
without our hearing it   to be glad   the rain
increases in the forest's folds   what is it   slight   what is it
that I can be there with you in mind   alone   quite
beside the bending-over tree the bleeding stone is white
travelling along the bedding-places are hyphae of fungi. Epiphyte or parasite.
After upheavals even our speaking is the thunder   symbiosis is tight
in love, derived, not quite   dried plankton, rain from old seas under
              where we stop to wonder.
Captain Cook's monument on Easby Moor overlooks the farms he worked at before The Sea:
now eyes go over to an ocean of breakers in new forests (of the North-West's slightest trees)
crows disrobe such sitka spruce, know them in rows, not to tide the weather
forever. Twenty-year pulp-trees   however it may go   mere breeze
raises on westerlies   instability had come to this :   command at fifty
but not past it : an accumulation of knowledge and persistence like a Cleveland hedge
round the Point for all of us   and back in forest watershed   the edge
     to true   the heaviest of the trees' condensation pines, redwoods, cedars
concentration   bringing low each branch to a needle's
          point
destiny   slow mulch   points soften
              to sing to make it sing under rag-leaves-blues and yellowing
the leaves
         needles turn pages   scratch out slow movements   with their slurred stir
where there had been oaks in Cooks time to build the boats   for England
some of their sway and pulse separating from their way
              in the wind not predictable
In the waves strong currents not yet known   not alone
              to make us what we know in boats in lines
                        and maps
and go   their lightness in my children's faces   studying so
              we have to say whatever it is that waits
is forest   and these plantations *haven't* waited for us
              they need the new dimension of the old
              before they're sold
as instant friendship, an affair, a one-night stand   needs sanctifying
from some found parallel with what has gone before :   you are the best

(on some slight test)   It's as though I've known you centuries! It's as though . . .
So we went on into friendship, navigating clear, noting signs:
'Rock Fall ', 'Lumber Trucks'
                    and
                          'Deer'
                            and then
'The Tallest Red Cedar In the World Two Miles' — thats some tree
and a mere   Hokiam
    screen of green between the Astoria highway euphoria and
'Felled Clear'   'Felled Clear'
         For tourists then and lesser men this road to this Aberdeen.
                              Dark grace to your snood brow
a mephisto waltz until the eagle dances : lost off loggers' rafts with me so near and eager
like bones stranded some charnel-piles to chide of whales the whiles I waited for your word.
I had not expected to find a Redwood so far north as in the Quinault, but there was one:
was it planted in disillusionment, meant Men? wild the forest otherwise down to the sea-edge
your peninsula   to know where you were.   Like hay, those logs,
spread in the wind from some gate posts open   you stress the last syllable as the downstroke
here in Cleveland and along the Border hills
of the extended black primary-wing-feather fingering at last lightly on the snow so
the tips lift first to test by touch the strength of the hill forests tumbled air that trees
ease into, stand on or lean on there along the Olympics and Mount Rainier, burst the
hayhairst and the birds
flying over, calling, cob of pen and anser, anser, Apricarius,
the mudrun and the miles of roads, bend-swinging stairs to stars
re-crystallizing ice from snows No Old Black Crow to fly back home to Ted Hughes
with the message of no passage.   This The Raven of Rainier
its rhythm every echo go   precarious oystercatchers
piping him ashore putting him in mind of his Atlantic and the Whitby North Sea Shore
tame birds, 'cheeky as a whore' 'putting him in mind of his first (1747)
              'Free Love' whaler out of Whitby:
words running in, dissolving like clouds into, the hill
              we all have a long way to go   still
to pick up on Indian words whether we can look forward or back
to see a trace of the giant we all have behind us   Quickhatch or Sasquatch
whichever
                              we met on the beach, the silent
stationery log-run of the West, the breach of etiquette
and yet

there was a slight earth tremor in the night
                              these plates we ride, the continents
move over one another like some discontent in bed together
being in a bus together near an accident we felt for one another but
each of us alone   cold   just jostled stone
going over this land together while we were still apart   we learned
the first laws of geography, learned by heart   love's earned
a new love by the analogy of the old   flow haar-mists at Whitby!
a clinging to itself of forest, fen, rainforest, rain
lingering as points of dew on Whitby ling!   The heather of hill-weather
and you within your shell of hell made the Northwest wring   your words out
and didnt sing.
'I tacked and stood in again for the land'   and offered my hand
(the going now being hard)
           'the weather being thick and hazy, I stood out to sea
till noon the next day, when I tacked and stood in again for the land'. My hand?
'the.wind veered more to the west, which made it best
to tack and stand off till four the next morning, when I ventured to stand in again'.
                               It began to rain
(Cape foul-weather) (44° 55'N., 135° 54'E.) 'Seeing no signs of a harbour
. . . I tacked and stretched off' southwest.'   Retreat seemed best.
'That part of the land, which we were so near when we tacked, is of a moderate height,
though, in some places, it rises higher within. It was diversified with a great many
rising grounds and small hills . . . entirely covered with tall straight trees'.

Those trees are screens now : for the reality within.   'Felled Clear'

Cape Flattery marks the entrance to the Puget Sound, but bad weather seems to
                                              have prevented Cook
from noticing the strait. On the Northwest coast of Vancouver Island he landed at Nootka Point
where the men in canoes 'could not be suspected of any hostile intention',
'showed great readiness to part with anything they had'
and one 'sang a very agreeable air
with a degree of softness and melody which we could not have expected'
'the word *haëla* being often repeated as the burden of the song.'

III Cape Disappointment

Dark strength to your snood brow, white baulks   your awkward glances
a mephisto waltz until the Eagle dances :
lost off loggers rafts with me so near and eager :
like bones stranded some charnel piles to chide of whales the whiles I waited
for your word   So Washington Irving's *Astoria*, chapter seven:
At Cape Disappointment, reads:
'Chief Mate Fox, ordered oft to land in the whaleboat
"without seamen to man my boat
in boisterous weather
and on the most dangerous part of the northwest coast . . ."
                                                                                        he was never seen again
What the birds flying over are saying : oystercatchers ostralegus, *Apricarius*:
     along the forest down to the sea-edge, your peninsula
                              Lewis and Clark found
     the Pacific Coast as stark   dark
     Sacajawea, stumped, driven to the extremity of eating steaks off a stranded whale
          the humped-back *Megaptera boops*   already blown
          by black-sand-flies.
                                   The place was mild but
     in Cook's log the place though forested feels stark   stalk
          his looked-for white cliffs (of friendly chalk) prove 'steep snow and white logs'.
                    In the company Charles Clerke, James Burney, George Vancouver
     John Gore   James King   John Williamson   William Bligh
     Molesworth Philips, American, lieutenant, and William Anderson their
          surgeon botanist and naturalist
                                   a man without a doubt
                                        (if Basil Bunting is the Atlantic
     Ezra Pound opened the Pacific with intent)
                                   until he went there
                                        (where desolution becomes
                                                            individual
          in the face of apparent plenty).

                                   There are birds feeding young at the top of trees
so tall you'd never hear they were there   the arches go only gloomily
rich in hanging vegetation, fungi if you know them well enough,

                                                       near enough to our own.

                          Henry Teesdale's map of about 1840 shows
The Olympic Peninsula as the 'New Georgia' and
                                          New Albion as 'New Hanover'
                   The dynasties
                             Wait
                                  we went
                          round the point and back
             in forest watershed the country up ahead   and felt
            the heaviness of the trees condenses power   brings low   a destiny
         we'd mistake for in our destiny   if we didnt know   what lines we go
                   events inevitable occur in Quinoet
                         there is a lifting-up to the present
                  we mistake in our intensity

                                                a climbing
not the euphoria of the drug American spurge   nor any splurge of
sudden feeling to the head   occurrs
                              still
                    the giant's steady step upon the stair
a bird in old leaves
             but, once, a bear   nose-in-air
blacked out the moon
                called me near as that once (Pacific) loon off Scotland
woke me its waiting in the Isle of Lewis
                                   Tarbert Shawbost as under Clisham
and here under Olympus
                       the effort still outward from the forests dead centre
as from some heart.
                                                  Sasquatch still walks
with Quickhatch and Quinaults and did I hear Queequeg
                         (the call of the night bird of the northwest)
waking up the forest floor   torment
Thor meant   some heaven   cliffs could realise
     as at Whitby   white birds on them
moving the shore   low shore,   with not even the wind astir
in Astoria   but it spins still   and all the hysteria is within
and its my breathing you can touch
                                  leafs these stiff oakleaves

over and back   over and back.
                            If I lie still   and stiff
enough to hear
                which are not yet too far down on their journey to fill
gullies for me to see or smell them   rotting here
putting their our warmth back on the air
they were made of
                    only
                        mean
                            pines resist.

                    What we had been discovering had been
some of that
            in their minds who so first named it
                            could I expect in a month an advance
on what Lewis and Clark didnt quite reach with Sacajawea
though the getting there had been remarkable enough
the communication ahead of them all the time
like the birds have by their calls or the animal scents downwind
or what they'd have us believe of old African drums
they went were they were expected and were received because of it
(the Blackfoot aggressor proved her cousin . . .)   and relieved
[to list and describe all the birds trees plants fish weather oysters geology
                            to sketch the characteristic
profile of every native they came across for an entire continent after the
                                Louisiana Purchase after marching
over the single range to the Pacific']   What Mackenzie must have read
  in Tlingit sign-language of hands and head
  after thousands of miles of 'only Indian say-so' and after even saying 'no'
  to the offer of a squaw or daughter
                            how we and his Young Men (about 10 years ago)
    went the sun's 'west to the Stinking Water'
                                lethal
                                    methane
'for the sea-fishing

white men such as he in two canoes
as big round as islands   and with white clouds over.'
Satisfied with having found the Pacific   within a paragraph turned round

headed back to Fort Chippewayan   knew these must have been Cook and Clerke
no silence from any bally peak in Darien!
            and Captain Clerke in the other ship, stood off :
less inclined to think   this must be The Inlet :
less experience but more articulate
                        his was the collier called Discovery
and he
'so far advanced to the northward and eastward' (remember they had opened the Pacific)
'as to be far beyond the limits of European geography
and to have reached the void space in our maps
which is marked as a country unknown'
                    their great design the Atlantic via Alaska
into and through the new cartography

                    we are both there as sure as bark is skins
this is the country we are always in
                        your eyes pigment these sea stacks,
purple   black   I am taking in
                        my first of the Pacific and in
your syllables you stress the first of the downstroke like the primary feather
of the heron's or the raven's wing.
                    Captain Cook's dialect
                            was Cleveland out of Border
the black wing extended full to its primary feathers to speak
and the tips lift first to touch the strength of air that trees can stand
                    or lean on
the mudrun and the miles of roads, bend-swinging   stars
recrystallizing ice from snow   and so we go
no old black crow but this   is the raven-of-the-longships
                            and its echo

[To claim the headwaters of the Columbia float sweetly down in triumph to the Pacific
after mapping all the interior]
                having discoveries made by Resolution
    that dont have to be pressed to any clear conclusion
        only to some Point to be Rejoiced ON.

IV The Inlet

                To discourse on the North Vest Passage / Insert
a large pork cutlet   inset in
              Lord Sandwich's dinner-party in 1775
        Cook   the first man to   arrive
and the last to start eating   at the outset *insight*
looking to left and right   still a north countryman, and canny
the piper there for his benefit as might *befit*   a heathen
    such as he   (he didnt know it)
retiring, a retired man   his weakness was in thinking anything was
not for him. They talked loosely so he would tend to get *in tight*
     50, but not past it   and stay there quiet all night
          in the revelry   (Later they
offered him flesh in the Isles of Sandwich   himself
about to offer himself)   They were such cannibals in 1779
        He'd stay *in tight*
              then
there had been 50 attempts already to find the passage from the Atlantic
Candlelight on the reddened wood and one or two faces (50 from Hudson's Bay)
        someone else would say
     As they talked,   the *lighting* improved
                   Cooks eyes dug grooves:
his mind already finding one ship, the *Lion*, then at Baffin Bay, minding
he'd need Americans, 6 of them in the *Resolution*
Charles Clerk : 33 : had served on both the previous voyages, for the Discovery
       when the good Lord's *lightning* playing about the house
freed Clerk then in jail for his debts   oh privilege   and they smoked
the Discovery to join them at Cape Town   and they smoked again
              and it was done
       Cook dug under brows less bright
         claret
           and the *lightning* continues all the night

It was how it was to be : just one or two
might have been missed, might not have combined as true.
In the Company brother Broughton, navigator
apprentice from North Yorkshire
                Charles Clerke, James Burney, George Vancouver

John Gore, James King, John Williamson, William Bligh, Whitby Chapman,
Molesworth Philips lieutenant and William Anderson surgeon-naturalist
        what is nature worth   not to be recorded?
he hardly ever had his feet on the earth.   He'd rather 'steer'
     the migrants song is near, only once in the year
          How can it be defined   if you think definitions are required
We have to learn to fit this solitude, not tame it —
I went back with a boy called Kirby Cook (with no problem
of the derivation of either name for him t whats definition?)
Compare this boy from Bremerton with Captain Cook
There is yet company where none intrudes. Not loving less, but nature more, for moods
if you would now have more : of woodland or of moorland or of shore
or of those pine stands we could together live out interludes no helping-hands
companions as companionable as solitude we reopen Thoreau at the amble
practically all his webbing stamped 'inflammable', his outward-bound expression
seemed to shout something all peace would scatter by. Of her green skirts the
                                          woodlands coming out!
   along a watershed, alternately alive and dead, the country up ahead
He made never a look up at the shatters of the sky
                        his splicing ropes, his whittled sticks
his rods my cones in my eyes make he   and he is coming
    less than she who will be ruined is woman
                        not me
project me through your eyes   arise yourself   my size out of mind
bitter only over us, better when we know
the effort all outward as from some heart-centre
beyond and from the Rockies off the Divides Cascades Coast Ranges
        range on range   seastacks dont calve
like icebergs do, clear ice fronts   or halve their dirt like the shelving cliffs
of East Yorkshire's till (tile black ships left behind) Oh Sir 'I'm sick for the cliffs
this coast is going bad' : the oystercatchers are all black. Oh She, she has us sure
Singing by chains the Ocean
                  swirling solving
posing in the intercross of ripples   an undertow
                   the questions row
like gulls in off the sea heavy with offal, slow
                        they know :
               they've been to the edge and looked over
and the Bald Eagle, dark with light points, steadily followed their whiteness in

round to . . . The Indians to Mackenzie had been sure 'this is a stinking shore'
   like the sea-cole shore of Blackhall, County Durham, rounded death
what the Brontés could balance from the actual recording of slow lines
: one sister in the kitchen while the Gondals worked out the geography
of Gaaldine, and all is mind and the journal is one breath

                                    We stopped
   to see what you have of steadiness, tree
   no less alive than no more than trees
   living-erect or long-dead on the windrow, mudrun, pile
                        his flag slowly unfurled
   where to the edge of the world I hurled
nothing is alive or dead : thats not the question
   rather, which of us is the way of life
                                the seas
this boy with his ordered adventure
                           the roll call and the grading and the
demands of his committed calling
and the traditions of the navy
                     urge
   the air, the earth of it, given,
going that extra mile   At his pace, first
      we all are if we aspire to it : ready to take on
         what the inhabitant is offering   then to answer its
look at the woods and the sky   the migrant birds fly by
                           he never looked up a bit
      too far to a blues for you!   He whistled country-and-western
birds and beasts of prey do purposefully   listen
              and their prey watch sky for them
even lazy reptiles stare
     There's something in the eye of all the world not half-observed
: a peregrine falcon's eyes are bigger round than ours
                                 this boy just worked
              to be at the sea.   What of The Ocean?
sucking through the rocks and sea-stacks   the sea
brings up our dead   rolled on

V In Quinault Forest

Waking up to the rustling leaves
       Saskwatch still walks;   as sure as his brother Quickhatch
                                                   walking up
walling up the forest floor torment what Thor   ment on the Viking Shore
of Cleveland, North Yorkshire : cliffs could realise because birds bred in them
    dark cliffs, though   black is the color of the inside going bad
they are there, such cliffs, *in law* of   Kwin'ot.   It's a drowned coast.
    Thin-skinning wind says to me, who made
  every place the same, every name no name
'I will make all new'
               without a word
                       and we
we heard   as with
   great puffs of sucking breath
the crown-fire leaps the short gaps from tree to tree
    in appetite   to make new lower storeys.
                  where they had to turn back
in upon themselves, dam hack   until the land ran red   resin-red
with its own substance   our outward insistence
tearing coarse calico   trees going
the mudrun pushes the timber together, over and down like sticks
       you know,
                the trees going so
     and then to find a lone Redwood so far north
a Californian   all woods are women
    trying to get away from California
                         What in a word is wild life worth?
        earth.

              With martens it helped, I found,
                      accidentally
to be seen relieving yourself
              we can put the idyll back into ideals
simply by taking the piss
reaching
unexpectedly
a certain level of communication   between us

the marten and I, I mean, we meant neither of us saying it then
never again
to be off the scent

      To skirt what we call is
           wind gets to where a man is
can still if it is rough run in his head enough

a people of mere messages on sweatshirts   we scream in skin as bird
and read the label :
    'SEE HOW WE REGENERATE RENEWABLE RESOURCE'

'Ripe Cones collected from
           pine trees already felled
baked at 90 for a week, then *how* they smelled! until the seeds
fell out through graders
       baked silver-poison against any raiders
meadow-voles and birds and any vermin you could mention in this war
and fungicide-coated agin any persistent aerial spore
        With all this new weight
          they'd fall sure straight   behind the chopper
(wind less than 5)

a silver-enough rain to bring bare hillsides, deep-ploughed, alive again
but only onto snow, you know : thats the secret   yup
its melting waters then, sets them the right-ways up,
      with such a start
they're guaranteed to germinate more than nature would
at 2-6000 feet
      But all the time we've bin waitin to take the air
that winds bin blowin the bared brown earth away
                  and we
will hev to move-on our pitch agen'

Stand after stand, new land out of itself
with the same schist, same wood sorrel, same elk, same clans.
Lodgepole pines couldnt walk continents like deer have done, but have come
up to the edge. From there its all an effort of our heart
on the still nest of night the forest-bird shuffles setting seeds out of mind these conifers are.

Shivery for bodies warm against their own wet.   I wake in sweat to
trailing drapes for a while, those epiphytic growths rainforest favors
                          for awhile the ripple goes on
                               its near enough in water
the humidity of green like an English water-meadow under flood
                                     not noisy yet, the birds;
time the noise seas through the trees
tide chains buoys and makes me one
I want to be   alone and here comes
                      alone
                      some boy from Bremerton
lumber
come, and I'll remember your interment, mother
to net a swallow
          make love to her on my grave.

                      Reminding me of the forester three days ago
'She was a mean one, that one; the timber that leant one way
and then fell the other'
               this boy came noisily
                        splicing the ends of ropes he carried as his fasces
a Temporary Fire Watcher
                squatting hightowered on his trail   a faeces
fasces change as faces
               animals
                  he hasnt seen any
                       while we're away the rain will say
Now I can strew the land with spoils for you
and she you'll miss, be miserable and true
the truth in feeling what rain seemed to know
                             Setting seed-heads out of mind
to pulp for red roadside mailboxes these conifers are
with such red squirrels Caledonian forests used to lay it on
story by storey, under-story : meaning so far
the tips were making, and no chickadees.
When the dark bird came, it took the squirrel, shook the trees
as one by one the chickadee flock forages through
keeping in contact with a 'see-see-ping'
teamwork, and no game   The dark birds dont bother such society

you'd think nothing had happened, nothing had gone
I had to point out the place to the boy from Bremerton
almost having to pray down on my knees
until the breeze dropped that eagle's primary-feather
we had to be alongside that, couldn't wear it in our hair.
Bird bigger than white-headed, Dark Eagle but no *iolaire dubh* :
the myth of Stikua according to Lewis Spence's
Myths of the North American Indians
                                        Stikua, son of Blue Jay
who wanted to fly found his first prey a young eagle
— a skin and spread too small to stay
                              on the wind when it dropped away.
So he went out until he shot the White-headed Eagle
found he could only fly downward in it, then only downwind in a glide
and could not rise until he applied his mind to it : any wing-seed
might fly the world if it only keeps getting up to try!

The one we saw got to us;   in off the sea that Bald Eagle
and you and me
the manner of his going got to us   for nature and all birds
Hunters ask me where my energy is from? I tell them:
D.H. Lawrence's thin   soles.

You know how it is with the Northwest: you can ride even a light wind
from that quarter;   the air is so much newer, so much shorter
places are that much nearer.   We have no word for it.

VI   The Bald Eagle's Nest

I'd met a man who'd shot
                        and he could prove it
three hundred eagles in three months
                        and they did prove it
and fined him for it, thousands of dollars
                              thousands of dollars exchanged for power

the reach across the straits the wild life took to men to stop and watch us
in off the sea that bald-eagle   and you and me
                        while he was being mobbed by gulls
and for about another hour   the manner of his going   got to us
nature and   all birds
the one we saw   confirmed our luck in love in them, their life.
The eagle to the naturalist is   type of the pacific resistance of noble nature
no less than lions really are
                       the real tough guys are weasels and the hawks
'the best of all' because they have to kill often and go far
                                        against the odds
     jut   cut and jib the air
                        the earth not laid open for them
as a table, but down tunnels and through cracks of air they dare
gestures for no other dare oppose talent
                        what one flick of a Falcon *talon* can open
what in a word, is wildlife worth
                       we have to learn to fit this solitude.
    What was it the Bald Eagle said to us
                wings mobile only at the writing tips
  and as in your pronunciation of it
          dividing the line-squall from the sun
                  stressing the last syllable
   something about how to fly   in the face of theme
In Lewis of the Hebrides there is a hill called Toddun
and you can see the eagles play with it, toss it into the Atlantic   then
with a flick of the carpal joint   spin across The Minch description arrows their narrows
to make the places speak   the heavy eyes of the pass, out of present highland peatpools
    Like Loeb giving the lines to Wagner
his confidence of the dark within us getting out   getting related
                  already in all our consciousnesses

'The bears went out of Quinault in the Depression : since then we've had no music up here'
      When the word comes clear make it come in here
         the migrants song is near only once in the year
                                    the next time they flypast
     silent, in different plumages
                         'the mooch is a slinky creatures
     minor and modal' : Mellers of Ellington's animal of 1933
the year they found Nessie first and since then we've been having Big Foot up here!
      Without the rain having to be seen to fall these leaves
    are wet with it
              as if the fine rain knew of you
     it had only to seep to make blue of new
                         translate for us
     into a language, since New Orleans, we couldnt understand
     but would demand
              it had only to seep   to seem
     and all its own reason would run through
     each drop winking its I'm watching you
              familiarity accord
it had needed millions of them: just one or two
              trees in cord
might have been missed or laced in somewhere lost
might not have gathered true
            as sly as you and I
                as seabhag to its stac
the whaup unto its merse
          they will be back
     sure as   kittle kine from the Spital Burn
row harme at milking time   at Muirburn.
This green is the heaviest green in leaf
          grief the most-insistent of separate colors
the extra weight of a fall of leaf brings down
pieces and bits for the mudrun and river drown
The same old story Quino: no god but just such thunder from the sky
will come by   if we wait why   this forest edge.
And who comes by?   No Quino!
There may be rhythms in a chainsaw but the Quinault Indian
knows to get it to fall so that it will bring with it one or two more
a good sailor can be sick up these high pines

                    with the sway of them
                                    But they'll come his way
            the Indian —   He watches the Redwood with me, glum.
            then, to find a lone Redwood so far north
                                                towering
                            They were going to bring it down.
            'Coast Ranges, no further north than Oregon'
            the books say of their distribution
                                    better had they confined their remarks
            like ours   to origin   Trees Walk
                    clouds race   this one is great
            from its tower the evenings wait, from its shade the flowers will be late
                                Is it
                    complacent of place? or even of times will?
                                                        nonsense
            the Arizona bristlecones are aeons older still.
            Not growing so you'd notice, no neat eco-niche to fill :

            your spread is other   sister, brother
            looking out on land   leaning each hand like a mother
            poking swirling fog   and penetrating our smother
            you know,

            'There are no end of Northern English in Vancouver
            except the Scotch

            we went south year after year   but
            only got as far as Seattle   that were
            enough for me.
                        We'd not care further
                            He *were* a grand chap, good company
            a raight naice fellow.   Didnt care
            if there *were* L.A. & San Francisco somewhere down there'
            The Bewicks Wren just heard that, rare amongst birds,
            but you'd see pairs anywhere any time of year
            sings *without* posturing, just getting on with life
            the whole life only sufficed to keep territory and wife
            and that was why we couldnt see him for a while in the Redwood
            poking swirling fog and penetrating our smother

to clear thoughts up about all this fuss of future
                your frass doesnt gather
                bothering the birds, the place's steady-up sap
stretching horizons seeing Puget Sound across the Py-ull-y-ap
wobbling on their heels such achoolkids on some trail who crane
Pacific-Coast *grus*, all Headed-up
on your balance-sheet of chance
accumulate to terminate in excrement in increment
                chance rules who came   we did
            where Cook and Company After had.
Generation upon generation
Possession is having what no one else can have
the view from inside yourself out   is not just even for the few
it is for you
           incest is bests leaves insist in bedding down together
even strict oakleaves will yield, putting our own warmth upon the
                                                                              air
    only after we have the trees down will the wood yield answer
clouds torn by the topmost twigs to fracto-stratus feel different in this forest
sorting out for sedimentation whatever it is I've leaved
              only mean pine needles resist.
They named the place, the inlet from the west   the place
they thought hope of home-harbour lay in best
after the place they started from: their slips had been built in
for the coasting trade in coal.
                    North of the Columbia, South of Flattery
East where the sun is *Whitby Bay* on the map of their contemporary Taner
how did they miss Puget Sound seventy miles wide, in their morning-stride that day?
The last word is   but we are always looking beyond the obvious; not seeing it.
There's no word for the Northwest except the Indian;
                              Knowledge is from the East but Wisdom from the West
(reversing European classical assumption)   softness out of the south,
out of the mouth of the North
                        Events   in Quinault because
forest regenerates from the outside in.
                What we were discovering had been
in the minds of those who named it first.

VII Aplodontia (Coda)

Rodent,   less than beaver
                              more than muskrat

Aplodontia

        peculiar to the wet Northwest
some sort of moist-earth prairie-dog,   no-tail.
Eyes and ears small
                as if not noticing I fail
In fact, looking straight through my life   a flail
for a poet feverin on
                how country enters in
who are we fooling?

he soughs at his reeds
                and he's in
long before I'm near enough to appreciate
                      on my side of the pond
his quite quiet mate.
Giving me time later
              to smile   at any rate.
Soft, sleeping under a wander of leaves in Quinault   and it ran, wind,
vallambrosing until the tap metallic   pinned latitude and longitude and time
and it was, this time, my Olympic Beer can.

Carcajou

a long-poem of an encounter with the wolverine of the Old and New Worlds by me and you, Hraska, Nara, Ezra, Erika, Sitka Andy, Alan, Cort, Alaska.

Carcajou: probably, French version of Okeecoohawgau, the Cree name.

"The form of this animal indicates great strength, without corresponding activity. The body is heavy and rather clumsy. The body is high-arched, the general figure drooping. The legs are very stout and the feet large; the track of the animal resembles that of a small bear, but it is less completely plantigrade … a remarkable broad band of chestnut or yellowish brown … running along the sides, the turning up to meet its fellow on the rump … circumventing a dark dorsal area."

(Elliott Coues: *Fur-Bearing Animals Washington* 1877)

who can face encounter   who must face it
listen in the forest first where the voices we want to hear
are not people's but of The People   In uit
                              made
                    out of the glade
enlightenment is sudden in the forest   eyes bright-red-brown-as-Mars
star for further looking level looking-in intermittent contact had been interment
you, Carcajou, only just recognised and before we know you
                                                  we listen for a tune
to engage being out-of-sight so much we require a ritual for a fitting-in
                    Dutilleux' *Symphonic Fragments*, fragmented
Le Loup might be so augmented
                              where you will be in our imagined-scheme-of-things
not hibernating, but we stop looking for light in the dark place we are in
the American dream-blight quick through every sensuous delight   active day or night
experiencing everything in a hurry   ahead of itself   the Fright
"omnivorous, the wolverine"   our starting place the Given Word
before we know its prejudice   Are you bear or weasel, wolverine,
or both   the space between your eyes is wide,   we all
to shallow graves you can grub up   Ours, are the animals
         evolution is the space between true trees
                    What kind of animal would you have been?
Trust starts at the eyes   and works in
timing   who ever does a bad thing, it is bad:
what is there   there   to make the word good
                         theres something animal in all of us
                         and a different animal is everyone
people and animals relate,   its one way into them for us,   and it must be for them also
                    one hero is one who
exposes himself where others watch, the only one willing to go forward for good
for others
                         No pushover, but   oh
I was mugged last time   but by a Blackfoot   or was he Nez Percé   padding away
I remember him though   I never had seen his face   (he was British Colombian anyway
where such things shouldnt happen)   taking away all faith in human nature
while renewing it   took my breath away   his belted bulk the wolverine way
Dont Stare Now: its not natural
                    naturally, nationality has nothing to do with it.

                    reaching beyond the visible
and all that takes our mind off what-goes-on.   The forest floor we walk on
carries all signature heavy self-consciousness "clawed, *vicious*"
(Don't look at me, for my forté   is taking animals out of other mens traps)
The first words in   having been in traps myself I'm through with them
until the next one
               This is a wood you increase by coming-out-of-it –
               out into the snow with a sawing motion of it –
bear-lope   muskrat-ramble   badger-trundle   marten-amble
                         the evolution we are in
is secondary-skin   concerned to sensitivity
with texture and with feel   the ritual further is
if you go, and with assent   (not to interfere)   the mustelidae exist
insist Rilke was wrong: you can point out a scent, weasels exist by this
not so much stealth in the stoop or the chase or the pounce   but persistence
quiet, laced there is taste in scent   stands on end when incensed
"consistent, lank, rather rough but generous"   this, of the fur
showing a little out of the forest   essential nature is in skin
              coming across to meet my   nervousness:–
an animal with a Tertiary look about it, somewhat unspecialised
                         individual and geographic variation
                    Celt-oval-headed, wide
forehead and wide walk; the eyes wide apart, the giant marten
the genes a long time rearing in the same pattern of creation
as the Giant Ground Sloth Darwin found; the Megatherium
something of it in the nature of the fur; Änne as if in the accent on her hair
stationary, evolutionary as stone : bones   rare, old, peculier!
an animal swinging in off the ground, never off the trees
                                   the mere idea of you
back-of-the-mind and building-over for years: on the wind the scent of you
so that eventually, after inactivity   out to the place logistics have suggested
            the game
so that eventually, after uncertainty, lame, rested in it;   we move, against the grain
            a name   just one species

Mustela barbata, viverra vittata, Taira mustela, Mustela gulo, Gulo gulo
Gulo luscus, Cub hylaeus, Gubo luteus, Cub biedermanni, Cub wachei,
Cub katschemakensis, Gulo bairdi, Gulo niedecki, Gubo auduboni.

Every carcajou is   conceived in the spring
is rocks out of the sea   is subterranean at the surface
snow is an anvil avalanche   volcanic
suffers so to deceive science   scratches   steps in ice
 makes everything around birth move   in its own cycle   motion
without our thinking of emotion
                              the eyes level
                                        energy-anarchy Viking-analogy
  each one once was on each own thing   (no registered nutritionist!)
watch cricket, bowls   no exhibitionist
wanting answers before the questions have been first
                                       the poem for our own marriage!
darts   there's nothing else to say, today
the Indian said   this way
"of this, when you have made it good   the animal itself
should that day materialise for you through different forms on the way, totem
             dream that way alone you know the way ahead."
Raccoon as   you have   conspicuous
delicate hands   beautiful!   amongst driftwood
 the bending greentwig pent-rafts   rigs the log against the sky
 why shouldnt I   go   on   twisting
                              the steady-breathing of the sly
means mean is   flinging the capacity for fun
           we play then, you and I   at last
                       come the same day as the sun
the animal, not my animal, is needed to pull us out, those who will be pulled
out of the present preoccupation to the new cooperative occupation
of the planet with whats in it
                    it has, as it had to be then for me, shown the way
the animal that has perhaps outlived its own prey-species evolutionarily
tertiary ungulates or super-rodents maybe – has taken us on a place or two
                       and its a contribution, oh carcajou!
"I only seem to hate, you see
                    because you will not wait for me
to say my say"
           "misunderstanding is ever the basis of your paralysis
your stasis"
                    anything itself beyond its dream
towers its own powers.

To be here at all now, to be here anyway
the animal has adapted to a thousand different niches
competing with wolves   bears   (including polar bears)
        fishers   – they are already their own giant-martens
        martens   (and so, sables)   foxes
        arctic foxes   golden eagles   great owls, what else …
the big wind and out of it   it brings you, it is what brings you
on its noise out of the sticks   which makes you coming   But it is not you
The wind is you past and the grasses settling again because of you, brushing
them wider, lower, harder than the badger;   and the trees are narrower, you brashing.
You are the racks in the forest and in the ice, the rhythm-tension that the wind
can only speak of even when it is breaking trees.
You have been, in your momentum over millenia the centre bearing down
the direct confrontation at approaching speed, head down
a blur, the line direct and straight-at-me.
You have been the difference between being right up to my insides, and distant
but not silent in the forest;   no, not that
or out of sight.   You are in the flourish, the stripe of speed along your side
you have been everything I have not known but in longer moments than expected:
a response
My questions, you say, have always had different levels;
the real issue so sudden and direct
it takes the breathaway.
        Chewing pastilles seeming in your silence, jaws moving
"winter warmers for fishermen   and trappers"   between teeth that nearly meet
dont interlock on them, dont masticate
        snout up, tongue rolling a certain trumpet
seen progressively as being, rhythmically,
        leaving a German symphony behind
we start to hear the forest organisation given-way to the organic
scratching the snow as the grass taking my breath away with my wallet:
No push-over but, oh, I was mugged last time, Blackfoot or Nez Percé
padding away I remember his wolverine way, his sway his belted space
        I never did see his face
but I should have known he'd built himself up for it.

what is it in your eye   gives enlightenment?   Cool company
              only intermittent had been contact   so far
until suddenly at my door brushing forest-floor
                                         the little muskeg's tympani
wind-string like the wolf-alone   your tone is   at the back of the mind forever
         where you are in my imagined scheme-of-things
is mime in time   Einstein: all time is timing   taught as   the wolf-in-pack
howls hack   calls circumambulate the track.   Inimically   imitably,
irritably   you carcajou listen to the ululations of the hawk owlwlul
what is it in your own eye   it is to-give   to become-alive
     looking for life light in the darkest places we can find
find some forest answers from within   hull the dwarf willow,
holler, if an advance on the invisible is immortal; your sudden appearance, Änne
must be good for you, virtue hide around the door   or behind a tree
knowing you will be persistent enough
                    beauty is all you see, and need to be :–
Darwin's "Facial Expression of the Emotions in Man"   span all we can
              anatomy has something to do with it
not merely the nurse's   though that is fine but the doctor's eye
Niko Tinbergen, by instruments we think you come   by convention   but
you call out just as we fear the snow   hot glacier
snow-in-the-sun   where we grow   who can face encounter …   Who amongst us
yourself to help you   on the go   along with the otters   slide in the snow
This mind the wood you increase by coming out of it   with a certain rhythmic motion
you say : dont you wish you'd know   my scent   in taste
my cunning   no waste   rich lingual lingo   accents lingering
you who, sauntering, fit my footprints as you go to come.   "You are older
but I am colder   where you beat trails I've been before"
                                              out of stimulation
              the evolution we are all in
out of a dark winter sky   to sensitivity is   secondary skin
                                    out of a glade a made
space in tall trees teased by wind   "I've shown the way.
I am with you often and I know you   you change your form to me and then we'll see"

Carcajou, it is you
rimming forest a long ridges I've been all the day   but night comes slow
emptier of heart than cold coming-on-my-way   the forest/voices low
moan   I would not say alone
                     feeling the light only penetrate
sawing away, chewing. I am a chainsaw of the woods that you   can sing,
cant see me through : its the co-operation thats coming in nature, I grant you
        Rilke is wrong; you can point out a scent   Enlightenment is man and caribou
                                                                 mouse and Carcajou
                     we of the weasel family survive by this:
there is a taste in scent   stands on end when incensed
persistence, quiet   (not just letting light in):
the wind does that from time to time on its own helped out in winter by an extra weight of snow
there is the certain rhythm comes in before you do (not just letting sap run):
the sun itself, forgotten for a while, with a little help from scratching badgers if the spring will come
               consistent, lank, rather rough, but generous
(this of the fur) merely a naturalist's description.   Not just opening minds:
like a thaw lifting blinds for chords and cords to saw   opening the minds
your way is just leading timber away   education is more than that.
        needing   naturally, nationality   has nothing to do with it
it is the place we are, whether we find it   neither near nor far whether we mind it
       imagination   (what figure, grimmer, than Grimm's Woodcutter)
                     the release I feel is your
(conscious of it are you or unconscious?)   penetration
         the old world figure of organisation   the ring I walk is yours
enlightenment isnt just letting light in   in the clearing
                     the wind does that from time to time
      I am for you this moment if you can take it :–
                                                    on its own
(or helped in winter by the extra weight of snow)
                                        prairie-sage to no old-age,
     not just letting sap run
dance to the sun this sundew, dance :   the sun itself, forgotten for a while
               the babes in the wood would, if they could   (with a little help
from scratching squirrels, badgers, vibrating sap-suckers   when the spring will come
                     watchout for wolf lest carcajou get you
               not just even   opening minds
                     like a thaw lifting blinds for chords to soar
               imagination   and not tradition

the old world fairy-tale organisation   in imagination what figure is Grimmer
than Grimm's Woodcutter   against wolf and wilderness cutting trees down over a continent
and then over another: watchout for wolf lest Carcajou catch you!

The land says   to decide
this scrap tin has had time   in gullies and in ditches –
since this land was made-over to decide   old cars are hard to hide
second-generation mechanician I am   not the indigene
that from the beginning was like this, adaptable   the so-called   Indian
whose trail we all must find   I sit a metal ridrind
rust and laugh (you've seen the oxidised stripe on my side!)
                                                                        laugh-grind
you wont find me here!
                         what you do   is look in the wrong places
              for luck   Carcajou,
After the Explorer
                   you run on old trails, unquestioning
After the Exploiter
                   you are left still unknown   and unknowing
After the Organiser
                   you are anarchy   "My Teeth Make New"
After the Hunter
                   and you only name a few though he is all of you
       I am still chewing through true, too
After the conservator   I am uncatered for, still
the eyes, and back-of-the-eyes, spell naked for what a lens would not tell
or dispel, but enlarge illusion on leaving like wanting to touch sway hips
the coat, the rank fur's thousand lips,   the points of the electric snow on them
show great stoat not naked fur
an exchange of saliva groomed across a distance   the cord running through,
the thread has its insulation before ignition or it is earthed:
to make a start, a stand, we cautiously declare to share the land
its a fallacy of our time that our 'knowledge' has us understand
so we can 'automatically' communicate, co-operate.   Carcajou, its not true
we are no more investing than inventing the situation, I'm not making you:
whatever it is we can say, differently, together, do and go along with
each in his and her own space and place so to be with it, strong with
its own reality, not its own image or abstraction, changing and sense
in the beginning a place-recognition, we realise after growing commonsense

in time and in tune I'll learn from the 'animal' and which is you –
what we make in our heads that is not new, never can be even, true
whatever it is called.   Encounter before imagination is in you, Carcajou.

out into the snow to roll in   my sight as if to say
(slowly you'd say it)   this is my way
tactile but laconic   I have already given you   more
in a few minutes than my cousins the martens did   in four years
            looking at you now I see you know
what in your wilderness makes me feel so at home
not comfortable enough not yet   you bring me naught for that
just so the hollow below the coteau's cotton woods dont hold snow more than willows
        After the background hiss :   this   this
                    is something missed:-
coming across to meet my nervousness   an advance on Ives'   Question is in your part-response
panting   parting fur to the raw-skinned wind
not humming some background-pastorals   your life has been too full of hurt for that
snout up tongue rolling certain trumpet   crushing consciousness
                    over away through the undergrowth
trees not violins, little muskegs tympani
                    like the wolf alone   alone   alo-o-ne
your tone is   at the backs of minds forever   in mime is time
Einstein : all rime is timing   taught us.   the wolf in pack   rhyming
howls back   calls circumambulate the track   the soar is climbing
away: something missed
                    you, Carcajou, listened
the hawkowl howled its lulled ululations   inimically inimitably
irritably   lull the dwarf-willow   hull   holler in his hollows
                    you say :
"I am from hiding, committing myself too soon   out of a species of fear,
but you are different   generally your type dont come near
you say dont you wish you knew   making-good the way it should
my scent my taste my cunning   away to
lingual rich lingual   the lingua franca of the ancients
lingo-accents   you who sauntering fit my footprints
where you beat trails I've been before   out beyond stimulants
out of a dark winters day   I've shown the way
what you have taken out of it hacksight hindsight deer-run bolder stood
Yes, Angiolina thinks and sometimes cries, as though the secret of her own existence

had been explained to her, or the secret of the universe in her own existence…
'Si, Angiolina persa e piange…? (last sentence of *As A Man Grows Older*)

I'm wide and low and take things slow
                                                awkward-shapes-to-honesty
my shaggy shabrack shakes   shapes   saddles with ascent to see
we can feed the rawness back into humility   subtlety   my entity
ez easy as Pound pound it out
                         as with the life of words
                         we preserve only to destroy, transmute
                  or first denature, then presume *captive*, found
what is it we try to cultivate   grasp at   as it were before it was too late?
what is it we are after
                 you, the survivor, know   though you are modest
                             I have some rest
our eyes met only once before you continued with your enjoying in my presence
as if it were *what I wanted to show you, I felt content*
I look at your lines, wait to breathe (such steam on this raw   air)
look down inhale look up but you're still there
without your image-from-the-book   with so much as a stir
of the negative they pin on you   'most destructive species'   'untameable'
at my table for this moment
             you chew cheap pastille!
                        there is a sense of humour
of control in everything you suggest   a species of unexpected-rest
most rare of the weasel family most fair you've been to me
so honest that I seem to have known you long   *trust* every little thing you do
trust every line of the song the pines are singing now
my face is space you can write upon   surprised by mud run   stumble into slews
if you can get through so can I   (no helping gesture though
       let nature make   true secondary growth   of all our inner forests
we will not find the tune without singing it; of the dark within a recovery
for all of us : the eye gleams shelter; any shelter is eye socket, occiput
the teeth flash burnish, across Asia spreads America, dead Europe head-on
(prejudice and academic expectancy) 'this is the most dangerous of the fauna
of the taiga'; yes, even if you count the Ussuri – forest tiger:
Änne, the beast is unchained in school, the horror is in anticipation
the skull maimed, the slash of the long claws' excoriation.

Missouri River-Songs '75–'77

For Benét and Victoria, of the unacknowledged flow.

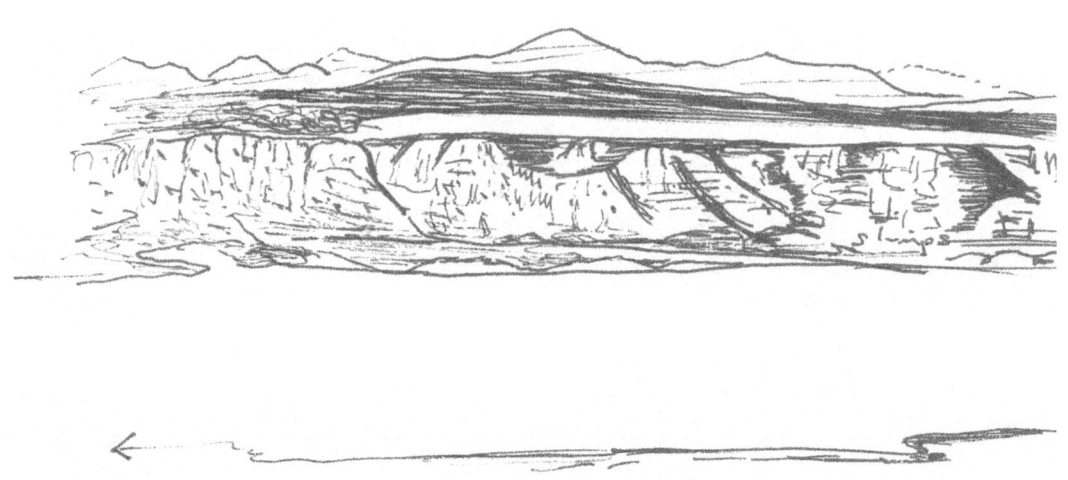

Mountains beyond river, and a high terrace of the Upper Missouri.
C.S.

1

Winnowing hawks   cleave air   don't push-aside to ride
ringing migrating sandhill cranes craze   morning's film
when they come to a merging with the place   mirage-playa's   crack stills
where the white-one will come-in   like a god-himself   prepared-for
visited as music as clowns for the turning on as of   women
rehearse-spring   deliberate prancing   a summing-up
Milk Lake stalk stark swing   to the strongest silent   singing make.

2

Farmingdale where   'Sandhill Cycle'   was
              if any there now they have to move around a lot more
re   a   rrange   its glory gone
Yorkshire-sheep leap the hurdles   days before   the storm
antelope, mountain-sheep herds would do the way they do   if there were any there
the shepherd knows how   the dead shepherd   the separate hills   instead
easily feels he's made the land   he's only run it   red.

3

Only one thing anyone needs to do a thing.
Why does a river meander anyway   wherever sea level may be
                  never mind load or substrate or all   the angles
it does so from its steep-gully stages   onward   down
this river   the red man said   knows that it can do
as any snake will set curves ahead of it to travel
smiling   on its face   the way   is ever-spreading   rundels.

4

Plain Man listen   dream
                                              bluffs   sway
their individual trees to each say
like the hills speak   teach   being illiterate   the blindman
to birdhood   shaking-cottonwood
sacred to pass   Greasy Grass sand and
stream not always on stream   but in process.

5

At the Missouri-River-Breaks in Montana
unrushed ferruginous-hawk flushed
bodgedrusty-finned-ranch-Dodges
came on strong same
song as ever long
soaring score
gone.

6

Milk River to the Yellowstone   we renew the earth
the hoarding said   after a little transliteration
if this is expensive education   what's the good old   ignorance worth!
Not by such navigation   but by   waiting-on the spaces
not split but by geography   by meteorology   by sympathy
'when the earth was young it was able to bare man
and feed him a milk-like substance'   (so, Zukofsky)

7

Prairie, the ripples run east   linearly
the roads are   far   too-kettles   early
                                    lateral-lines the fish are still   finned
                                    well-dressed protest will   be skinned
up Detroit's safety-poles to ring alarm-bells
scampers this campus-mouse

8

No picture but we can be sure the lip   the mark of *Falco*
has at least a lateral notch in it   (Crazy Horse's)
         … the upper mandible has the same serrations
in all New World galliformes and in them only: it's from distinct-instinct ground
none of the Old World grouse have   (whatever their relations)
so Ridgway taught us of the corpses on the gamestall at Store City
in the grass it is written plain   for whoever will pay attention.

9

Lake Sakajawea made against the rain and thunder's will
that can rinse this road   or run that riverload
as anyone forced to fill   old space again   no leeway left
for my seasonal spread   winter   bereft.
Sacajawea (Lewis and Clark's guide) was her name   it   smelt
sensuous names   to be writ felt   in water
at least once a year is season's melt.

10

                        Harney's sun   Raven
                                    spun, soaring
          my high-mile Harley
      gentler feathers   underscoring
      how small the holes the best adapted make
      to dig roots   build homes   chop wood,
                                                            give and take.

11

                    Crazy Horse said   'Don't weep for me
(Lakota)   if I should die in war
Don't   look   back   at   me   I was before
the reality I went into is the world is set store
anyone can go there who remembers me to forget
himself   for The People of Their Place.
                              Do not regret.'

12

Everything wants to be
to make
round
their landscape is because of going-round and round of itself   (horizon)
river-stones, water-drops, wind-dust to made ground; alluvium, loëss
'square houses are not good enough
so no spirit will stay in them.'

13

North to South the grain of the land   the good-wide-roads-between
Sierras   Rockies   Winds,   Horns   Missouri-Coto
white man's clearance   worse than the glayciers-made-go
cleaning the grain of the plains back way the same way
nature (the received) will fill   vacuum
shortgrass   longgrass   pronghorns - horses - buffalo
take down the wire fences   so they will come; come and go.

14

                        stuff   bloods
                here   where   the   bluffs
        are prairie-squared-off-wood.
      not tidy-plots entirely but squared-off-hand graph-paper-grand
          is-this-what-the-land   was waiting for?
      not hiding-grace exactly   reared-up, stand   trees planted-in-sand
         is this what life is coming-to?

15

Wolf-spider   frenzied-purposive   solely hunting
     of the ground only   stuttering   *Lycosa pseudo-annulata*
the grass unzipped by such lycosid spiders nomad-thing (Wyoming)
crazy-spinning   coarse-silk shuttering sheathed-shallow-holes, hinged lids.
And the Jumpers *Phidippus*   leave little grass-leaf litter   mutters
brief lives   hunt down the soft-bodied insects   themselves destroyed after sex
egg-sac shunting   with writing on it from turf for.

16

Birds' plode heather peace   as   hear the old song gong-going shepherd on Esklets moor
wide-places filter   long spread   what's said   gong   what carries   carrion
crow the tone of the   conversation and not the words   a man's voice-over   void   avoid
still as   headlong travels herd-long over calm-water   over a mile
without the hills throng box   vox populi   transmits   Dakotah
avoid   as what   harries
the wind is within strong.

17

Eyeball-sky   everychange suddenness   stimulus   cumulus
see the little clouds off the   Bighorn ridges   run
running-exaggerated-speed under the high cirrus the sierra's eye cirrus
meniscus like the puffs of industry power-storms edge   puffing   powerstation
not significant at our distance   stance
meaning nothing   but putting us in mind   (chamber music, to Sibelius' 4th)
the little clouds are there to make us laugh.

18

In the long term of energy   endogeny restores exogeny   that's oeconomy
the exterior waste of the earth   is renewed from within   with germination
his bones   the buffalos'   the gophers'   to grass to asters   to aske
to red-willow go   or creamed-off-sheet-flood   lodge molecular   lode
particular generally looking through ridge because of what's - this - side that oecology
picture-assemblages of forms regenerate lines   will in his visage   engage
the fact of the country passed-through is as genetic as ours   that's phylogeny.

19

The coaltip-look of Butte Montana   Victoria
and is this what this world was waiting for   depreciating
                    stone stripes line down the spoil-hill heaps of home however new
its the timing and the spacing   that matter for   understanding appreciating   strew
align   lane   the course of life-strain constricted in the bone
its stress   the stones in the stream say so!
the holding music   as the grass walks   through you.   As the grass will.

20

The moon as red as the sun   and as big
as if some perfect perfectly-lonely   cloud   signalled the sun's setting
ahead-of-time the   Indian of the Rodeo
but a steadier red   gelled   it belled   sounding
looking at it through the distorted lens   of the rim of the sandstorm-earth
powdering-underfoot blowing   all of a sudden there is a warm wind
Benét   air-off-the-plains   every breathing cloud   brings down   breasts blessings, land

21

The face to dance on is   not always recognised
the Northern Steppes-loëss   the graded-down land
not ground-down, urmstromstaler
the frenzy of knowing   'Who You Are'   with atoms and stars
                    the rhythm of walking is breathing the wind
the vee-twin beat   clip clip   clop-clop   clap-clap
only the earth stays   only the earth   even if, even it has lost face.

22

A happiness to die for   a felicity
the subtended hunting-ground   of territory   beyond
space beyond   so you know its necessary   to be dead
                                              piecing together sane and heather
                                              thyme and sumach time and weather
                                              to check war for youth and confer with age
                                              him and his kind fight by heather and sage

23

Any spirit that's alive and working still
adapts tactics as a shadow on a hill
careers not as the cloud that cast it   moves erratic it
                      the ruse of the faint-retreat
                            certainly in themselves   committal – sureness in leadership acquired
required he the master of it   had his horse dance to it
        to … fuse the force through the ground green in the will.

24

Though it is washed away   though it is blown away   though it is sold away
there's wearing down   mounds edge the town   cut sod just rots-down
and there's wearing back   dust storm   distributes black   claim map maim hack
the long bends spread   we walk blown-over-bed   they talk in stead
spits for the red-willow   the river dune pillow   contour-despising furrow
gray-brown-black-red-yellow the-night-it-falls-back-on-us-so quickens the cycling below
only the earth stays   *only the earth stays*   *only the earth stays.*

25

I cannot be but to feel   a foreign body-short-of-grace   anywhere upon this face
but cannot help but feel   the long-call dance the reel   that rings the place
makes it one waved space   contouring
the Eastern Meadowlark sings-from-the-rail   the Western Meadowlark sings-on-the-wing
sail, fling   do not fail or fill
the sky a mind each day   a daily bread and breadth   the breath to bring
man so small on a long, long hill   and the evening canting slope a cantering still.

26

I never knew him or his kind   in at the creation of the world
but we can all listen   not a vacation   inactivation, I have the dream again
I am where it is morning   I am walking   in New York   but it is there   from O'Hare
                                                   on the Reservation
and until I see their faces I do not know it   though I feel it   in the air.
Any man of action   needs his   has
       ages of, in, attention.

27

Syntax is a tree shedding   wet   sentences
on tip top or a taut-tent   teepee in the gusts
that come-on sudden-after-rain as if to shift the drops.
       In the great cold-in-the-teepee   (January) concentration drifts to great-gain
        for the poor man and only he   to open the vision he who'd let the dogs pee
         against the skins   not wish them harm for it   spoke agin poverty –
yet save all wintermeat   blanket time   which is all anyone gives, in rhyme.

Curley Crazy Horse: always seen in youth with the Younger Hump-of-the-Oglâla
you have to be in a certain way with a land to be (out of hand)   held
given familiar names   like the Norse (off-course) gave their fields   fjeld
Curley's sheiling waves its grasses more as if good nature the deer preferred it …

for a stream to a cottonwood bluff it seemed to be always smiling …
MacDiarmid at Langholm and the love of place was first in heart
artificing is Black Hills berry-picking …   on his own in company, sticking.

A Celebration of the Stones in a Water-Course

                              This
the most successful image   of the warchief   against the Wasichues
has left us no Picture or Character
if we like we can choose
caricature   'The Savage Cataract'   which cannot
be true to likeness.
We can lose him altogether
canny.   In his shores   contrari-dictu
there's no-one here   though this river's cataracts are like his rivers'
White   black   water   sky   sentimentalise   abuse
in time   the blues   fix the land where his colours didn't mix   whose
going only   RED ROAD   WHITE ROAD   BLACK   Black-Hills Custodian
approach by a braided-stream   the only offer of use
SENTIMENTAL LOSE YOURSELF   BEFORE YOU CAN COME AGAIN
reproached my proffer   I will ask   permission

I found the Badland scarred by watercourses
                                        too small a land-base for The People
inadequately served by any transportation
                                    dependent on an external administration
pride-of-being unemployed hands worn not to perform
                                    warned Welfare's effect on soul-flow
choosing in the absence of Education   the form   of the land.

Urra Moor in Yorkshire stride swinging   Pine Ridge heat haze ringing
dancing disturbing   rumphump   white-feather flirting birds
in such movement the rider   runner free sees between
the larks sparkling   there   out of sight   in air
the pipits starting   from our feet   startled ringing
there aware as consciousness on two levels, the sane upper and lower frames
playing Sioux children breathing still crickets shifting their gaze are singing

Fermenter meadow-lark the first   lowly and essential   snowbunting second
lamenter of winter   crow and magpie   third and fourth
prairie-falcon and eagle fifth and sixth   any migrant dove seventh
for heaven   and finally the man-messenger   cut-serve sent
along his own ridge for the moment supine   his inside black
and then I needn't wonder how it was you said   MacDiarmid
of the Pentlands   you 'didna tak walks noo, but ye ken   I am not dead'

under the river of intermittent cut   into the earth   not pushing aside
half-inch flatworms glide
sun old in moisture   they flow warmed stones   rounding as they ride
lubricant of time   but sun slow dance slow   pick out his bones
whose burial is known   but unknown   as any plews
somewhere near enough the creek called Wounded Knee   slews
are turning over at last   in revolutions   as if *he* hides!

the slew, stained slain		the man
turning over at last	he lets sinews	between them stress
re-learns the suns caress	as earned dues	hands
relax to his sides	eyes open to the blue	
wider ripples register	turning slow paths of flatworms	
warms to them	will watch where he puts his feet when he gets up	
not to harm a few		
not by considering consequences	he knows what he must do	

basis disregarding faces' emphasis on their way to waiting – chrysalis larvae metric
mere creepers but they shake heavy grassheads apparent sticks stirring looping geometric
on their own bearings cantilevers hesitating before launching out to lay down bridges
measuring the earth   pace out   unseen folds as if they stretch brown ridges

The man whom no amount of foul-weather travelling gets down
the wolf and poet in one who feels the pull of a place like Berwick town
standing on its river   Tweed whose mind   feels round   draws all things
is drawn by the little bluffs of nervousness into usefulness   proud to carry
the scars on the body   and mind   they are for the land and the people

Like waiting for to run a long cross-country run
                                                                    ready to race
space   in isolation   there's irritation the first hour or so
                                                   then melancholy sets in
to hallucination   is no abstraction   its the real world we're in

the spine zero of what we've all waited to see
the feeling drawn-out   meeting   the ministry
insistence on out of the cold left-handed handshakein tension
as being   the extension   *nearest the heart*   the immediacy of old

jumping, crickets flash black, red yellow the choice of roads
thigh muscles expecting to be sore : not an erotic set of skin
but   panic wet   sorry   sweat before the event
you do ... do not ... sell the land our people walk on

the walking hoppers wait their renewed migration

the walk, the long walk   what Parks are for?
but blind   the reduction to the will   will go beyond   made land
stars dont twinkle   their light is constant   no instants stand
our minds just turn the switches   dont understand

spiny thin thigh muscles expecting to be sore   before
they are asked for   He was the first to notice that
I've noticed reading in athletics   c.f. Percy Wells Cerutty
whose methods were the sane badlands repetition   and then more

Cruel and. Kind at the same time   *to realise the real world beyond*
most important the lives up ahead   *the future fences*
left unsaid or until you are dead
                              there is no figure, *no likeness will be taken*
the mark of the hawk or the falcon.

Upper Missouri always the same because changing its land, browned off: cured slow
hunting said stop now, slow, this is   land tired even before its snow

when he is not, in the nature of things   feeling tight with the cavalry
Tashunka Witko of the dancing horses with his knowledge of shifting water courses
preferred to be at them at his own game in the summer but with his own tricks
chopped their uprooted winter tree to little sticks   denied
his motherland's nature laws out of pride   even to fighting in the night
                 tied to season   not knowing it would work out right
whatever the eye sees stands to reason   but to go beyond sight
while others, thick-soled   dont go off on their own   value only the tangible
dont tangle with the subtleties   or practise them
this is the basic division there is amongst men

                           if you can be sure to change direction
the land isnt going to stand to attention   its going to take you in
never the same two minutes running

no river of no return is saying   wait for me
he said dying   *dont look at the past of me*
                         not as the river runs less, the land lives more
                         cut off carved ways you've never seen before
Upper Missouri: Upriver Song where you know you forget to ask how long
the river bends time all the time left hand from right hand

```
                                        if they are openings to the other world
so that we know it real
the opening bars of music         to a Steppenwolf        and these are steppes
with red Missouri wolves          along their breaks      not Gray Wolves either.
Seeing something in a suddenly-different way after a hundred times ordinary
red as read                                    there are no such things as accidents
picking up a man's mind     in a book     no accident I must have meant to do it
```

'Wilderness' is not, wildness is not to the likes of him, it is all the lore he can give it.

```
there are places all of us know when the brave man stays there agin its sale
where we do feel alive enough     I do not want          to learn it from handbooks
want to learn it from being on the land    on hand       Dreams
Whether it mean travel to Vermont   or Asia we want to be Emily Dickinson's
little boy                                    like the hawk, shot on the wing
murdered at 35 years old          be he never so bold
yet certain I am of the spot      by the rhythm      o' it as if a chart was given
```

```
The White River Song of many melt-time tributaries lines all twisted so the derived
cannot be distinguished from the arrived      and the native doesnt matter anymore
or relate to the land he is from.      William Alywyn's Elizabethan Dance no. 1
in a modern rendering anticipating the run of the original
is very much like traditional Hollywood 'Red Indian' theme rhythms
(like they play just when the long line of warriors breasts the high-plains crest)
In menace rhythm makes moods      phrasing       tone steering trails
a man on rails is rearing mainlines    felt and felt-manliness     the snow-melt
my heart is full of blood but not pumping            repeating at each undulation
after the writer in each head, cussin      cover sun          cousin behind
and the flirting on arrivals      to my dead whose snakes are out
seize on old spinned-off cast skin
```

dead   turn up   scale their own   circlet moons
stroll circulate-breast-plate
the burden is on me to make me   *where time will find me where before*
no one has been   before   and everyone must go different
                                                                     offering

(lieutenant) Two Moon (Cheyenne) succinct of (reported) speech
(it is not that I am weak)   the Winds (however they tweak)
wreak nothing on   *I have heard the coyotes asking each of each*
when the spirit was on
the sun, is what they're on.   The moon by night.

The Missouri breaks.   Braided, the land slips into the stream
isnt what it might seem   leaders, after the issue : seam
it is after the flood that the runoff   has to decide on which channel, choose
the Sioux have too many leaders   for the new Wasichus

Gravity ultimately gives spurs bank undercutting at the short laying down on the long
with cut-off slopes beyond bubbles undertow like clucking bones only once-song
back up backswamp feeders the slip-off of the Missouri   Coteau   the leaders
we wanted to look at War Cloud's paintings like hanging about the Telford library
in Langholm for the shout – from the rivers – bones you mix with tobacco and once only

shown shorn by the too-late sun waiting for the song by river, the shout
Christopher Murray Grieve that sent you out warrior also out of Langholm
where the books were to where the books will be : in your own countree

        Not those nob le sa vage, orn-a-ment
        trans-mits blinking steady star, what West meant
        the con-cept we carr-y is Con-stant the Stranger

        down to whom it all is now who said
        go beyond rue do not rely on memory
        if your eye is goodness and you are
        look a-round and you arent in danger

not getting stuck feeling it dirty fresh rainstorm Missouri muck
like gritting-tracks   sweep eyes   Missouri freshet breaking *embaras*
air whisper   ing   out   deep earth because of the water logs stuck
we lift our feet diff-er ent   the loft-snow shoe flat   right bent
in mid-web pattern making for dancing master fording   bare-arse
'those yards ahead are reality thats the real world the rest goes on without you
like Naylor at Catter ick cattlegrid his long run a cross England said
'really getting into a run like this is concentration : to finish the journey is it'
a nose like Wordsworths for head down and breathing easy in the wind

Some momentum but the pendulum in hail   Smithsonian Institution
a path – describes across the floor   the way we are going round
the east follows on after the west   this day Si-nin
the Chinaman crossed my path   as Li was to   to keep the circle singing going
China is not a threat to the west's internal economy'   Two-kettle.   Sans Arc

if there is a place outside   in frightening wild things
then the thing that hurts most   will be pride   wind sings
in the place of sand   Bad Land Flirts   Red-shafted-Flicker   wings
open-ground woodpecker of the Great Plains whose wing and tail linings
show red (as against the Yellow-shafted Flicker, red whiskered agin the easterner's black

the mesh we are all trapped in   is the richest web   there is
Everard Flintoff's riders across the Steppes   old Steppenwolf
stepping out of place into it   high-stepping   are riding
west to origins   like the Indian reddens in the eye of the
taxonomist   (except where he's been burnt by the wind, he's brown)
but the birds do well to show red, some of them, everyone in phase
with the seasons   Red-tailed Hawks   Red-shouldered Hawks

                              in long distance   races
       the runner committed   gains places   by doing nothing
       by holding pace   when the pain comes on
       in the marathon   this is somewhere beyond the first ten miles

the song of going is a long long song   open land lung
leg   heart   arrange the terracing on the page and
for the voices   benchlands are for resting the eyes   on
you have to run the slippery backswamps slews or take them at a canter
to make headway or keep footing hazy its Crazy   But its dancing

                    Do you see   I had to go on foot
            span nearer a hearts-task than further bare necessity
        talk-to-myself more like a long ride than a walk   this is a stalk
        some creek called blue to some Sioux   between head-lands all
        are the Niobara into South Dakota from Nebraska   look away Sante
        stock-truck to within two days walk of Pine Ridge   to the South
drawn into the mouth of the nearest draw until nightfall to miss the roadblocks
rednecks and blackbirds call   walking wherever there were indigenous Wheat-Grass
the boot my moccasin preferring them their fresh coarse-caress   Buffalo-Grass
the constant Ten-Mile-wind made velvet of at distances   Gramma-Grass
stepped-terraces of waving arm of hordes — last seasons' seedheads, frass
stood slant the swards sinuating swales scored once – watercourses slashed
now do you see   I begin to
                                sandwaiting high-stepping horses or on foot
grease bushes and occasional cedar   the way to feel it
twisting run   long-tail weasel   to the Creek called Wounded Knee
to be aware   avoiding   to meet at my feet   cracks voiding
a trick learned from crows   the old enemy   flying home out of sight of guns
along convenient ditches   carrying for the eye   fine map of the whole country
                                            then spiral up the nesting-tree

only to have the whole nest shot out from underneath

       look away Sioux-Santee
                      the freshwater-east-sea Cree
                                          and Ogebway
look away from me
                    to the creek called Wounded Knee
                                  I felt sway
on the April already haze   cold and the gramma grasses glaze
at some 30° from the vertical   not like I've seen them upright : cycle
a stolen night's steady freezing fog on the North Yorkshire moors
                                      slashed by deep cut dales
badlands are only opened lands of other richness   erosion exposes them
fishes fruit to museum sales   fissures you could hide an army in   he hid
but thin   milking the Milk   and powdering the Powder
the Teton where in summer it is the flowering Tansy
winter is in   powdering underfoot, blowing   naming parts
in tune to a flooding's rise and fall   growing now levees each season
of a sudden there's a warm wind   and there is singing on it.

All facts are omnipresent!   Being proud but not pompous
feeling like a foreign body anywhere   optimistic
learning from the birds   or those of them which flute
like the dream of Goethe to command the transient.

as far as the pin-stripe poet as plumbed
                            celebration   Waste Land Deep
if we dismember the seasons
do the new-life plan when the moon is coldest
work out the hibernation   by ignoring the big sleep
push ahead *through* the snow   to no particular   destinations
we will remember   *Remember it will come after me*
because of me   *but not in my way*
look away, Santay   expended in Doughty language
extended rivers expose their ribs   reveal
                                        Cypress Hills to the Osage
an anatomy   as in Arabia or along the Border Hills
of another age   in fine drainage   texture
Bad land topography   is a maturity.

Crazy Horse's bones   round out as   sticks and stones   as little hurt
somewhere near enough the Creek Called Wounded Knee   the sound is heard
as the suns melt overgrow the snow   in April   and there is a sudden bird
oracular, finer than   a   bronzy   grackle   taut   as   a   bison-coracle
bobbing about on the air a rattle   as lasting as a dinosaur's clavicle
as divided in interpretation   as any nation or with reservation
such as kills   spirit   in investigation as in their education

At the forks of the Belle Fourche there is no evidence of glaciation
the angled geometry's too neat for any complication in the geology
such violence is swallowed-up in the land of the open-hand
and the place of sand : they say there are no right-angles in Nature

We have to ask ourselves real slow   if this sun-melts overgrow
has made a lynx of a bobcat show   in the tracks. In the traps we see
Stezaker's stiffening physics & stuff   made sceptical but the aim was enough
long song the Sioux Brulé-loess clay   when out of the wind and stain
chalybeate with iron the spring plays   patterns repeat cuesta the grain
the same as on the Northern Moors   laid down under gritstone bluff
the snakes and frogs are red with it   the whole tan runs on   free

Sprague's Pipit: 'In the eye   the sun
                    I am
                              in the sun   I am'
the spareness of a wanted-way
not of a wasted fruiting-opportunity
                              such humanity had
                         has all religion in debt
                       to the pipit and meadow-lark
                     looking and listening out of the dark
              for the fewer words the better, the more the bad!

alone against the sun at his nodal
reasoning for strength at any season
waiting-totem wondering the principle
cultivating rage violet back of beyond

                                      the inviolate range against the sun
                          Cypress Black Hills Horns Tetons Winds all one thing
                     attentive on outside himself in the pride of his own being
                      on two levels the upper and lower consciousness
                  no likeness but these shadows growing to the west then
              coming on from the east were his first identity in vision
            walk in what comes after me. The Standing Rock of no inscription
          second cast sharper as a marker should shadow stabler starker
       waiting for the circles of essential learning-will Young Eagle's darker
     than the Hawk upon the wing and his chart shows the Badger's extra dimension
   down in plains earth with the Weasel of the Day for the Dancing Horse to ride on
and Crow Dog and the others of today revived the live low levels for the head
and heart again   as if grain   kinnik - kinnik offered   ferment
fever to wait through winter and summer to what in his head meant
wind
spirit
awareness

```
                                                            hard to shout against
     moulding     plane-off    terraces      hold back hills     supporting draws
                                                         spirit
                                   the hills ruffle the wind        re-make it
like the easy-lope walk                the tussock-grass            to spring
pull at the back-of-the-knees
                        up the scale          freshet-sands
                           of swales          benchlands
                             through hills       clench hands
                               to 2-moon mountainlands
                   maintaining two red luminaries     sun and moon
                   sun-go and afterglow
                                   not facing things too soon
the turbulent reservoir of air and stories is
                                   not little ris' not just spread sky
time bruising all directions at once servicing wild raspberries not slipping by
bad spirits hot steam willy-winds singing cypress stems       shaking
red willow stop thinking        not drinking           slaking
late to life   late to melt   but for man with the plains emptiness in him
necessary time to brown off                    Brulé : the French for burnt
feathering the Bighorn Sheep                   stock-still as if they werent
```

                              feedback
                     Milhaud's La Création du monde
                        Milk River to the Yellowstone

when the earth was young
it
was able to bare man
and feed him
a milk-white substance   but by awaiting spaces
geographically by meteorology
where there are no roads   we can spread
                and it is never mind the iron rail and never mind the road
                    let us make up the old trails and pick up the old load
                                 the period before you know
    whether he is wolf   bear
            coyote   wolverine
            or dog   or badger
                                 the period before you know
is not the time to go   to the green dark forest too silent to be real
like some dead men   who steal silent in the night but real
renew the earth   unbind the steel
watch the floods   watch out   wash out the roads

                              geometry;
                                             the subtended hunting-ground
relates to the pictures on the wall, the cache, the style of the narrow pound
and the level places for gathering wild turnips
                                                    his seed lies dormant
whether we rake the ground over for it   gentle violence   or not
                           carry the skin is thin   land hand map
lost in the sense of wandering in sunlight
                                           for the sunnier side of life

its his cruelty real enough   but most of all the taunt on horseback
reddening necks with words !   song !
                this so called reality is wrong
                                the Viking strategy of the feint-retreat
time after time drew out the sting of the enemy
                       Concentrate on the principals on your own stage
    the character animals totems put there after the visions
               and see the pictures flow   the richer with age
    the right roads are some of those seams on his visage   the badger put them there,
    the long-tail weasel, the spotted eagle and the sunlit air
    rainy day people all know how it hangs on a piece of mind
    at the centre is a spirit   dont deny access to it   give it off the first to find.

       'beat Colonel Reynolds 16 March on the Powder withdrew west to the Rosebud
beat Three Stars Crook on the Rosebud June 17th withdrew west to the Greasy Grass beat Custer
on the Greasy Grass June 25th withdrew west to the Bighorn Mountains eight abreast, victorious
tree and stone spoke but Crazy Horse had started the singing anticipatory on each occasion for us'

                    at the forks of the Belle Fourche
                    there is no evidence of glaciation
          all violence will be   swallowed-up in land
     only the land lives long   ride even the massive landslide
        they say there are no right-angles in nature *between me and Great Spirit*
is no *Great Father*: wouldn't even go to Grand Mothers Land with Yotanka Totanka and the
                                                    Hunkpapa

The geographical centre of manifest destiny is neatly near, just north of the Black Hills
south of Box Elder Creek and the Little Missouri where Wyoming South Dakota and Montana meet
southwest of Slim Buttes northwest of Bear Butte   the place the Oglala called Two Top Peak
the little breasts   with a prick for each scale on the cone
truncated at the centre is a spirit you who can deny it   that's what you get for loving me
a uncomfortable alone
unstable
alone
In the eye the sun   who when he's cold makes fires for himself
I am
In the sun I am

    Sun   scale swales   hills to mountains   the way the moon is up amongst them
                    dry dust   red as the sun sometimes
lured Custer into   lined Medicine Tail Coulee   gave the other troop water enough
Reno's enlisted are still drinking   Benteen back to his butte with just one canteen Ogla la led
an   Chey - enn   Sans Arc   Minne   Con   Shy éla   Santé   Brulé   Blue Cloud
  Hunkpapa Yankton   to where behind and beyond   the inviolate mountains ranged
reared Proud, hon,   read proud,   real proud;

ruffle the wind, remake   the back-of-beyond
the Black Hills, the Horns, the Tetons, the Winds   carry noise on, tell it
not just little rises in spread sky   tales
the appearance of cold-kept dead   with a turbulence of tails
late to come to life   feathering the big-horn sheep
all the time   torment the hot man plain emptiness in him

always clean like city lights at a distance   but never spread out, bent-away
the arc of a bow
where time is bruising from all directions   at once
        not dipping by
service   wild fruits   hot steam sentinels   pines   stems   singing quaking asp smoke
red willow   stop thinking   making
breathing is slaking

                moving consternation sun-motes relaxing Concentration Blue Cloud

steppe birds are rarely gregarious   but for migrants
                      sense   the roots of Buffalo-grass
are a great mass matt at the surface not separable from their neighbours in their patch
for anything up to twelve feet down arid dense
                    what mattered to the people was space
                    tense   the hunting ground
around   it was too silent to be real
for us
breeding now beyond nineteenth-century numbers   being the breathing-space West
in danger of the descent of too-many leaders   higher types nearer extermination
as unwilling to breed   because they are for the Nation
                                    there were so few of them
only vermin teem by the million   Higher types breed slower
"I would have loved the Aztecs and Red Indians"   I know they hold
the element in life which I am looking for   … living pride … true blood
            … All the rest are craven'
                              Black-bow in the sky of Montana
Cooper and Hemingway riding slow below   only rifles

                      needing only extraordinary environment   until its ordinary
       ordering independent

                            the big vision is to be clouded in the uniform

                              The threat of National Parks
                eyeball the sky   the ever-change   the sudden-ness
       putting us in mind of the storm-basement   the cellar   its feel-and-smell

little clouds of the Bighorn ridges running at exaggerated speed under the cirrus
the real cirrus like the puffs of industry back home in Cleveland
not significant at our distance but putting us in mind
like the relationship of chamber-music to Sibelius' 4th
                           the little clouds are there perhaps to make us laugh
pare to the bone   but   mute

                          at Sisseton, Café of the Four Seasons
                              the pie labelled   I was told 'Canadian'
not so much crimped at the edges as   spot-welded
                 sunspots   across   the sun big   disc

            Blue-Cloud = Arapaho
            summit of Cloud and Evening Star   cumulo-nimbus
      rosy on the just-darker than Japanese skin the thunder-spirit, thin rain speaking
Horses dancing in a ring over reflections darkling on mud wet fine sand re-
distributed aeolian   we see the sky as it is (for him
as it was) if we see it beautiful. To be alone for. Like feeling the black girl beside me
on the bus, her smile
      takes-short of the platform : the locomotive 'Nimbus' broke down at York
                           to a stop

```
DONT WALK     was for the crosswalk          walking          (laterally)

DOLTS WALK

                         the cruising black girls plump pumping knees –
I was walking              and not whacking
                                    the cruiser's wedged cleavage
it could not be done          FEDS     pester     PEDS
                                                objects
                                                of suspicion
what I was walking was the grid
I discovered              slipping into it for convenience
off the highway      down     onto    rusting rails
the death of socialism
               in America               cheap gas




what would have been an advanced system
of electric    public    transport
```

                                                            Los Angeles

                                        At
The Missouri River Breaks in Montana   unrushed
Perruginous-Hawk flushed by rusty bodged finned Ranch Dodge

Wanblee   Galeshka, Buddee Golden Spotted Eagle bolden float
in the sun   the noises   otherwise only wires'   underscoring
                                                      we got wise
after highmile   milehigh   Harley   on Harney
speaking   fear mother thing   after Crazy Horse
                    a thinning of the atmosphere
                                        south through 120° east
droop-necks whooping-crane cycle   spark undercarriage-feet

slow-steam   vee-twin   beat
                    then the feathering for the induction
delicate the little corrective quiver
                    second-stroke accomplished at 4100 west: the plane
                    of even, breathless deduction
deliberate into the low-sun stun stammer
                    in unison   barrage   the singleton
                        shivering hands   up eye shimmer
       of Galveston   you point out how ricelands
compress
delicate upstanding grasses waver after their passing into scansion

                            slope-off   north
                    completing the hoop migration

               walk the streets of this Indian town today and feel
                              gooks leering automobile graces
the break in the chain   the damming off of the braided river
               bluff wood planted to break slamming wind and pattern of slopes
only encapsulated. links in these stickers books and the other lines in the faces
gazes glazed as in pain
                       in wild places   only   wild turnips wasting plain
         there are a lot of children   some of them enter
      chewing rosepetals and buds a rabbit on the steps of their Arts Center
inside Red Cloud and Gall   dominate rude red road between small walls
     outside Peter War Cloud's wagon drags a few looks delivering his paintings
    up the hill an athlete panting the only face still red or pipe-stone
          aloud on house purple as thundercloud owns up rusty-wing bird
            Brewers blackbird highmile Thunderbird hawk over   no city

he against the assumption that we cannot know the hunter
mind   history   god   share
because it has been bare before summer
forty   thousand   years   bare
ochre painted or the natural stain of the grain of the place?
so that   places I have been in   mind
Urra Moor   Moxby Moor   Box Elder Creek   Greasy Grass   must be left behind

Blackfoot   Minneconjou   Oglala   Brulé
Sans Are   Two-Kettle   Hunkpapa   Close the circle

hierarchy only apparent at time   the rites of spring split ice   crisis
                 high and wide and the higher and wider
to have no advisers is to be free as boys : because only a little band
                the more explosive the break up is
two buttes – twin peaks – a big one and a small one
             in twig   in water   and in the mind.
When Crazy Horse went to the place where there's nothing but the spirits
that was the real place
                                                                           Og lala
happy when a thunderstorm is coming : some one is on his way
                              when a bird drops   someone will die
sheared-off on his own
                                    mind   shared

                 there was that burnt smell of a dead bird

        as he made particular the general vision of dancing horses of Black Elk

        we must dissolve the particles

                from Harney Peak   Black Elk described
the g(eological girdle) 'whole hoop of the world' but any place can be the centre
it is the centre with the flowering tree that is so saved. And then the rain.

I've heard it and had some sympathy with the view   that you
                    the National Parks represent now
more threat to life and liberty than   the rough country before.

In this attitude which letters to The Times recently and elsewhere   underlined.
By and large we enjoy good individual relations with *individual* lands
and we should jealously guard these   dirtroad grit   teeth
only the earth stays   only the good earth
but here it is changed   lost face

                    at the edge of   and into
eating mens meat too   first the sweet
things that they had   like wild plums.
From here the gleam doesnt seem   to be moving   at all

snails-trails in the Dirt   the Missouri Breaks
repulsive to farmer princes   takes

the prize of water   to corporations   Ouse-Ure takes

       itself   the clear-success of the distance – tilled
but the river isnt killed   leads   Sundance-strips-cut-out
attached of the breast or the back

                                        the cut-out shaped-place
in us which otherwise had been for god   now he is absent the hollow's the face
for security   for beauty   despite barrages isnt   going anywhere

rootcrop and grain
no gain
    in the thunderclouds thunderheads rain
and the flood broods bud
flowers its own food
water stained with fresh fields
for Downriver
profits drained of year's yields this once-over
make the People bigger
      you get to a place at the border
      before thirty or before forty
      where you are alone
      the rest is cover
looking for patterns in the descent is
lines associated with a woman   masturbation in badlands
Moreau/The Bad tomorrow the bed
White River Sands the woman whose face you've seen before
and nothing seems to matter any more   done
dunes because its trackless tract attract
the music in a grain of sand an angular pyramid itself
the quest; mirages   are a simplification of it

Not in at the creation of the world   I never knew his Kind
but can begin to listen   (not a vacation   in activation
to hear
of a sudden there's a warm wind   and there's singing on it

only men of action
need long hours of inattention
if you've been not-giving them
                       I'm glad
their Cheyenne River is our Good : their Teton is The Bad
piecing-together   sage   and   heather
felicity   is weather

*   Do not regret*
*   do not look back at me   I was before*
*   the reality I was in is world-to-set-stare*
*   anyone can go there who remembers me to forget*
*   himself for the People of Their Place*
*   Do not regret*

        Thunder
for every cloud that breathes brings down
assent of blessing on the land   and on every hand   that stands
after the rain or the thunder word   *the land is happier.*

Parflèche

Written in the head visiting Rosebud, Sisseton and Pine Ridge 1973–5. 'Theatre of Seasons' Café, Cashtown, on the Whaupeton Reservation, and then re-written in Commodore Hotel, St. Paul, Minnesota, October 1975, and in the Scottish border hills of Peebles, the Tweed and Lyne Water, January 1976.

for Victoria

'The People are free. Its the proudest boast. Any of them can tell you that freedom is what makes them People and not fraki. The People are free to roam the stars … asking nothing of anyone … A fraki is just a rather repulsive little animal. But when they say it, it means 'stranger'.'

Robert Heinlein: *Citizens of the Galaxy* Ch.7.,
New York, 1957.

'Greet the People: that is what Lakota, Dakota mean'
                   Leonard Crow Dog
                   at Wounded Knee, April 1973.

Section 1

Pine Ridge walking down east to the Field Museum, Chicago.
30th October, 1975.

Mind my takin' steps to yer singin'?
                              Coming faltering mind
down from Pine Ridge, starin
                    past all the way to O'Hare with
                                        seeds burred in coat and hair
What I had learned there   about birdsong   staying long   holding the note.
Wonder, it starts in   singing   swinging sun
happy to have been there   tiny hamules and hooks and barbs pulling out skin
toward the cycling sun   they dance   is *rejuvenation* renewing the note
no wonderful thing can be achieved within or without sundance
                                    a mechanism
Sprague's pipit endemic   singing it   without knowing it!   cricket's wingcases
I want to hear the children   singing out of their epidemic *education* a song fluttering along
buzzed in the Museum Hall   which has been   still in Illinois
            faltering in   bussed from Zootoma   stopped
short of me at my bones   where I was 'waiting   I hadn't been waiting long
    when one of them with 'How long you bin studyin jest animals?
                    Do you know about the bones and everything?'
they had watched me as I had used to watch the dark-suited come and go, limping
     under the white man's desperate burden
                        in the Field Museum in Chicago
                                        not this, but the basis;   land
'Is the Totem Pole still growing
                Did the Indians bring it over from India?'   'No, from Indiana'
'Why dont you know just by looking at it;'   'When cant you tell me, Mr Man'
'Why dont you know it just by looking at it'
                            I started to say
        'You see   we move, so we must have bones'
  To rattle them, get a tune of them aged by their infirmity, mere bags of bones
                                The aim is song, I told them
       sold them the poems for their ears   their ears at their sticks of ankles like crickets
socks down
           no wonderful thing without its mechanism   The diaphragm of hearing:
the feet of waders and singers, hitchhikers, Burrs, Clingers. Well back in Wisconsin
                                            the aim was song
         that day until I overheard just such kids say
                            because there was water there they'll build their

                    atomic power station by the Black Hawk Lake   Koshkonog, against the peoples will
          and I   remember that Barred Owl in the Minnesota Valley
                 sitting on the Sundayed bulldozer, waiting for the earth to turn up preying   voles
in the face of privilege *prohibition*   asserting manufacturing rights.   The Hall of the American
Indian
the teacher one of them, but as on some head bold assurance sits
like the 'fifties walks on English hills (in shorts, big boots) they stride the marble hall and that is all
'Are there wigwams on the *Reservation*'   & All fall down and Who's it?
   (Southeast again and the Mockingbird down in Ohio : OPEN HAND
             made as much sense, didnt it
                                    each sentence is a sequence of notes
                       A game on OPEN LAND
              at some speed even a human ear can appreciate   they are sentences
     all life is
              each sequence of notes
              if we forget our insistence on rhyme
          detract free range   Homestead Act tractors   taking away their range
     I didnt feel the breadth of it, hadn't been, until I had to walk out of Wounded Knee
to miss the roadblocks   the tune I had then   and cannot now remember
     except its at the base of what I write now   doesn't matter   because we knew
          we begin to know rhythm, recognise the moment
                     we mock ourselves by waiting
                                             you sang well, she said.
What was the tune?   It had come of walking over to Pine Ridge from Chadron   calling
along with owls and red-necked blackbirds   not, this time, the red-necked Goons
                         how often we think we've heard the knocking at the door
there were no mocking-birds, though there were cuckoos   and on the lakes north, the   loons
       this bird we've heard once only   is here now   and by calling it
we got the supplies into the besieged.
                        Go away, they'd said at Rapid City, BIA,
reeling into our own direction   leaving at our own chosen speed:
              no point in anger : man is not the ruler
                         dying   and more
the various Indian prophecies, corrected against calendars agree
on the Renewal starting somewhere between 1863 and 1868
                                        what was it started then?
    Makes the mind go back or seem to : twice before I've had these feelings

```
knowing there was something missing
                    By an Irish lough, just waking                open to
all the stars winking past expiring
                            the loons calling had me by the shoulder, doombird with the
hand-owl of ill omen hooting
                    hearing still the call that woke me
the near-human crying of  the seals.                    Other birds
sing best at dawn or evening.
                    Then, on a barehill in Wyoming
eighteen years after staring                                      at stars
in the stirred cluster, sharing          howl       twilight with a coyote:
          uwe           uwe       uweeee       uuueee     ooo      eooo
                                now please don't misconstrue
the near-human crying of the hares
                    as made me know why


                                        I sing, and they do
Hiawatha's words to seals and otters : the White man will learn to cherish you
to his followers     the same White man will have you perish

GLENVALE ROAD  :  CORONADO ROAD  :  SAFEVIEW
some tire tracks in sand                some posts, miles from anywhere.
No Horses.
                                    Road names already up
                                    over the sage-brush, and in the scrub
BE GLAD TOMORROW YOU BOUGHT LAND TODAY
BUY COUNTY  :  GROW RICH IN GOOD LIVING
The bag must have been the earliest invention:
the carrier-bag for carrying out of the supermarket of the world
to the collector, hunter, fruit-gatherer.
```

The trees are beginning to look self-conscious, such trees there are can live here
PRE-DEVELOPMENT PRICES : INQUIRE AHEAD
and, after a little distance :
WATCH FOR CATTLE : OPEN RANGE LAND.
                Taut as sealskin umiaks
whose sails of ice have gained composure from the wind, content from land or sea
and gone along-way toward a perfect land
whereas Kit Red Fox dragging his rabbit   or even, scavenged venison
          is nearer the true figure of the Red Indian
the way he does things, wild.
                Whose bag we are all in
           Par-flesh
Custer put his head into the bag
      alright
         along the Greasy Water, Little Big Horn
            murmur of waters
knowing no tide before economy
         the carpet-bag
empty of good earth
         Panniers, Crazy Horse filled his
not with ammunition but with air   and some meat   deception
travois in the rear   to travel light.

Section II

the girl was a Swedish reporter to Wounded Knee
who wouldn't have got there if it hadn't been for me
      me   being reminded of   Marilyn Monroe
we by-passed the BIA and the roadblocks and got slow through to school
stalking   hawking   talking of
Mable Morrow who reintroduced native crafts into the curriculum
of the Plains Indians
like decorating the parflèches   their travelling-bags
to revive the arts
      to develop 'viable' commercial applications   and
      put some flesh on the bone:
'to demonstrate the positive qualities of the preconquest   ugh
Native American way of life'   (J J Brody in review of Morrow's
      Indian Rawhide (Univ. Okla. Press. 1975
      in *Museum News* Nov Dec. 1975 VOP 54
tough for the Indian had been, for example   No. 2 p.57)
      the singing in   Sika Hollow   of one species
tittit: breezy shreeee   unique
pica (peeca)   peek   tictic
      tit   tittitt   sheeiup   yee ip
yeeeeep   speenus pinus (spinus pinus)   siskin, of the Swedish Linnaeus
'This is my prayer. That peace may come
to those people who can understand
an understanding which must be of the heart
and not of the head alone'   (Hedaka Sapa: Black Elk of the Paha Sapa: Black Hills)
      The goon we met said:
      We're feeding too many people
these days who aren't doing anything
      an if he won't work   I say
feel sorry for his family OK
      but let him starve   I say
teach 'em skills get them off the reservation
      Anything else is subversion
      As, at one place on the way,   (Ogallala 18m)
the rebirth of day   sky east the clearest washed-out blue
    and Rosebud pink simple at first then slightly flattened   ball
    the geoid sun   the insertion of the sun   in the frame of faces, 'sickle,

      slanting the bars   twisting the flat earth   in our progress East
      slowly drawing the colors out of the land   hanging on the lid
      bringing on the id
                             a grey period with each bar
      finding new veils   ajar   -seeming-to-be-dark again with
      flowers on the east-facing verges awake   black wind breaks to dark green
      planted pine in a funeral evergreen   reminding me of carrigeen
in their starting-up
      sun to eight-figured in the bars   still stars
               caught for the day with her hair-rollers still in
      shy from duck eggpoles take on linking wires
      this is the way the awakening has to be
      the sun at a hands breadth above the horizon the October browns
      can be distinguished, themselves : the corn, the cotton woods, corduroy-plough
      (Nebraska's Reptile Ranch's) weathered boards
      the beet at its elevator darkest & lightest piles in the landscape   husk
               less wild, more trammelled but back more travelled
    hush   the Union-Pacific railsides rusting from gray   in the ray
dust-mote HUSKY GAS   red-dock district over red-brown grass
dust-motel still silent   The sun now 2 hands high
    but all the fur on the land, and the ducks over it   Yellow UPR
    the golden Coteau dimples
                         and divide below Sprague Pipits
stuffing the air, stitching it turning it round   Hedaka Sapa
     the mystery sang alive   in the singing-birds   flying their name, the hills'
the Black Hills are foursquare   they say
              East : I am higher than the Coteau, better hunting
              West : I am of the Rocky Mountains, standing stout out from them
              North: I am Black waiting for the white
              South: I am the last sun before Night
The Dead Lands are juxtaposed   and the first life again
              the Black Road is not forever now
                             just suppose
the land is people
the sun now 3-hands high : the little fleeces in the west are flying
Sandhills Cattle and Incomes Tax   Chieftain Tourist Village

Recolonise the old abandoned lands
                                     the cutover, Blownout
and the lands within the mind
the soils that have turned to sand   blow, blow
that Americans need to know   by the agency of someone else
doing the feeling for him
                             (Gold it was, brought it out)
      Custer stirred scandal   in Washington   all the admin of the Western Frontier
      grafts exposed
      the name of an Indian Agency or two
      Black Canyon Massacre of the Sioux came first: Custer has been agin it, but came too late
                     went wrong whenwhe got a P.R. man: Mr Cambadge
                                   of the New York Herald
                straight away took to taking an Indian girl with him
in what was then Montana Territory   Col Marcus Reno defended Custer at the subsequent
                                                            enquiry

Lakota   alkali dust   Did they want to score against us
Custer on Indians was right in this: with them you don't do the expected thing
                                          The goon again
       they ruin & wreck homes, the federal houses
       about 2,000 of them   I think
       and we spend ourselves and our lifetimes for them:
                                          as in your Ireland
      Shoot them to pieces   it'll be all over
        they're on the same page, (the same place) as the Singhalese Liberation Front
Crazy Horse   positive
      'have faith in my future: it is no use now to depend
on anything that is past in me.'   to his father
'it is no use now to depend on me anymore'
    (dying)   let us forget him to not forget

Sprague's Pipit is the short grass air-filler
                                and thats a lot of volume   the song has to
withstand sand-wind and old melt water-strands
and still stand up   and I whistled on my way
like there are millions of the flowers individually, but each one of them is small
even the posies of the Yarrow *millefolium*, bucket-fulls like sweet puff-balls

bright as they grow along waysides in England but less pink
do it all by individual brilliance, I think
                                    filter the unfilled earth of the giants white bones
weathering-out in gullies where they strode slowly   dinosaurs were giant fowls
and they knew about place like Indians do.
For messages at Wounded Knee   we called like owls.
The past has gone toward the making of not every man
                                    and for every man to do
not just look back upon.   Sit down   stare out   and
stand up and go forward to
                  the beginning or where we were again
strangers in a strange land:
                       what did I know
                                and I told the reporter that I'd learnt
that what made the pipits sing in the morning was the same
that made me whistle.
                           Good Earth and   Bad-lands
          is this the skin of the Creator:
what news can it carry   to the penetration of alarm-clocks
and the stopping of super wristwatches these naturalists all wear   sand
tors in the gritstone of the English Pennines and the   sandlands of the North
                daunting dry strand lines like lines of Hebridean bog
                        white
windy summer   hummer   mosquitoes   are only diurnal
                terminal civilisation:
                       by and large they are
the least adapted peoples   are no peoples:
everything they have done has been cruder   only their minorities
(since the Hopi) (and the Navajo)   are hoping.
                  'This is my prayer.
   That peace may come to those people who can understand
     an understanding which must be of the heart
                    and not of the head alone' (Black Elk).

The sun rose on this Sioux shanty-town and its high-noise of noon
as trains trailing railing   the plains too far away
                           and the sea in a mirage of brown

so whatever it is that will come soon here it can never be seen in town
no hunting but the concomitant-sitting-about   how under this hunters' moon
the people will survive as folk, the last Indian   in town will be no hunter
of the open-space no listener even,   poor-will or loon   though his will
might be snapped as clear as a sapling   the winds had down
                    The church pock-marked head-high by bullets
but the sweat tent (temporary)   stayed rock-steady   under   it all
            and   the owl-calls.
The idea of religion is foreign for us
made-money of life as if it was all   or a marten being skinned back toward the head
                like in Siberia they put out food to lure
the marten at the prime skinning time   its not our way
               as if it was all, all lived for, the rhyme
of their seasons marked up 'In Account' the hills, all hills are ringed round by singing artillery
    We are all related

                                        'we know we are not Indians
            Only Indians are Indians;
                        they are not metaphors but men
            we learn from them... and discover in ourselves
              a pride in being alive and a love in being silent ....
              The "spirit" is returning to us
                                    and we return to the spirit.'
                                            (James Carroll
                                              Contemplation NY 1972)

                                    understating, going on eroding
the dead are not powerless:
                    like   'the hills only are forever'
let the painting speak.
The mark of the genus *Falco*
is the double-curvature of that upper mandible
                                    is in
all the best portraits of the sixties chieftains: thin lipped
but the gape running back   as a sabre gash
skin texture at 390, hail on a gullied Big-Horn Outcrop
Paul War Cloud's portrait of Red Cloud
in the Póhlen Gallery, Sisseton
                    says
'I have a little land left:
  the spirit has told me to keep it'
                        it is safe with this
face to be seen again   with the coming-back of the Spring
like the Peregrine Falcon at home, for all our poisoning, and the Prairie Falcon
over the Powder River   is strongly on the wing
wandering but with a nest   *Falco peregrinus* as *Falco mexicanus* heckles and stoops
        hekhek   hekhekhek   so far and no further,
    Wounded Knee (1890) was the end of the Frontier
                        Bird out of the cliff
                            something died there
                Bird went back into its cliff for a while
    Wounded Knee 1973 was the start

                                    of something else
                                is it Crazy Horse's heart
                                who would know?
        The Sioux have too many leaders

Sisseton
                                                            (20 Oct. 1975
                                                            for Renville)
                                        palliass:
alias
Bonnie Prince Charlie

                    pretty well   to the approximation of a culture

                                        Crazy Horse: there is
no picture of him, never was:

                                        alongside the road they still have
these artificial slews   for snow melt, presumably
sex is   the tension I can change
to a torsion of perception   for the writing down of it
the pattern shows   the vallum inside the Roman Wall
here as there road & rail is parallel

            the high plains are thin : the earth has a lean
            cover of short grasses or rock patina under a weak
            and a discontinuous soil
                            the air, the snow, the flowers
                the scents are   thin.
                                    It is not the cleanness of desert
but it sure is the Divide
        temporary houses from the permanent
                                clearness of the arid
ration day on the Rosebud   a cowboy proverb for the wasted
            the retreat of the dispossessed is
                                    a climatic

                    there are no laws in Nature, only Privilege   but
                                                        the rednecks are early
          in the inevitable stages of   the reservations will grow beyond them

Deerskin Dumped in Dustbin   put me in mind (Salt Lake City 1975)
no narrow rubbed in to preserve it at some rivers-margin
                                                  its blood clotted at the edges
                         Kee Waytin
                                     wind
                                          is the loneliness inside of us
let it in
          never mind cutting the mistral out: as too opposed to comfort

irritable   Table   like thinking of a dirty Indian
exhausting like a diesel
                         no-stone-bowl   but a plastic-stem

the activity on the wind is endless to us
                                                            economic
                              the man of the future
starts with this skull   of the Indian
but will he survive agin less civilised people
                              the need now is for the gentler tolerance
Megalomanic seeds
               Custer's

acquired taste for raw onions and his
                                   needing a song for the 7th Cavalry
when they were forming and there was still gallantry

                                        he put his head in the bag, alright,
                                                                      he did
that he did   and for   the entire   7th Cavalry

    it is the People that is Rights
            standing on the Roots

one room, going to school is one room:

           where the only law is Right
           you get only ever less

       half of whats called 'sex' is this togetherness;
the nearness, the nearness of not just of bodies
          alive and warm

we've dressed it up, all right.

    white men : white 'wasichu'

    just as there was slavery of blacks by blacks in West Africa
before the plantations here and the black 'wasichu'

    there was war before, *between* the reds
but there was cooperation also in the hunt and jealousy
    I know where the best herds are; you'll never know Shyela
kept a tap shut

             breezy shreeeeee
unique
  pica peek tic tic   tit tit   tictic

shee i up   yee i p   yeeeee u p
flick in flight the flash of yellow

         Spinus pinus (Speenus peenus)

                    Not the tree-creepers: a man's clasp on the tree
                could be pretty   but is not eternity
earlier, not just in time: peopling old interstices by spirit ceremony
                                                    In 1969 there were
just 44 left; I mean growing where they grew : did the Indians bring them
over from India? and
        continuity means re-birth

                                The trees will tall grow again
                recolonise the red abandoned lands:
the Cutover   The Blown Out.

and the lands within, of the mind   the soils that have turned to sand
                            will organise again
Bad Land (new, post 1860) I mean)   somehow
                                        someone has to do the feeling
                        for the Americans
the Oligocene Playa-lakes   (White River).
                                    Deposits in the mud
the early Horses preyed on by sabre-tooth-cats
                                        It'll come back to that.
Wyoming. The Dakotas. Nebraska and Colorado were Great Plains then
the little lakes of the fossils, temporary mud on them.
                                    It'll come back to that
                        it isnt so much that time is running out
say scientists   eco-scientists   to all the 'world's echo
or materials or   ozone   or what-have-you
                but the cycles coming full circle'
                        but we are getting back to tribal life
they roll like rhinos   the buffalo   and they turbine so
men with heavy forelocks will be coming back into fashion   because of them
cant keep clear foreheads   and they are coming back
tame enough to ride among   but not so tame   as kine   and they'll be wilder.
                Bones vertebrate our way.
                            Crazy Horse to his father:
'its no use now   to depend   on anything   that   is   past   in me
and he died:–

have faith in my future: its no use now to depend on anything past ! –
        not forgetting him, we dont forget

Asians are the Far-Western Indians: Columbus was right in this:
10,000 years ago, 15,000 you couldn't tell them apart
those who came over then
and those who came brought to labour on the California railroads
running red westward now, the rusting rails of West Watts, Lost Angeles
'the suns coming back North
after the earthly revolution   that seemed to exile it South
back along the "red road" the north south direct path in Sioux belief
....'the suns coming back with
       life heading in the direction of purity
a natural way sacred to the Sioux when thaw heralds the spring.' (Altany)

         In Sisseton I
           stopped
'sparrow sings winter on the barren land   (R.C. Halla)
       but the tips of my arrows are sharp
and I will keep them so until
       sparrow is buried in the mud of spring rain'
emergence from the unseen centres of survival   of the cities
especially the Mohawk of New York   the Omaha of Chicago
Sioux and Chippewa of Minneapolis
         Herbert Read said to me that at the riots was Anarchy
like the Missouri gathers and rolls

      'predictions are seen to be coming around
         out of the ground'
Red Men To Take Over Again
     Indian Country is Coast to Coast

        the winds will, off the plains
confidence is still
       this is the contrast that will fill.

Rushmore Inhabitation

An Exploration of Borders

```
              Turning thunder                                              Turner's painting
                          prayer-wheel                           spun off sun
                                   somewhere between
the Western Sea and the Pine Ridges with men talking only electric gadgetry
to be in a place where they were not and we were
and because the grasses sang so steadily
ohm on the low resistance of their frayed-points passes man
ne negative steady pad me positive electromagnetically induced hum
as if badlands camels come                              education a leading-out
                         somewhere between
nature trail and      where you unburdened your tree           present: me
I learned                                                      to shout
              Thunderbird* you heard
I turned the corner
              Circling bird.
                         From Navaho territory
                                              [like me
from shortstack near enough to Flagstaff but] with no comfort
of no wheels
                they came back to their own
                                      fifteen hundred miles.
   To Victory Cave the Cheyenne remnant came
                                      the winter of 78-79
    one tenth of them or less
              the lesson of bird migration is there are no lines on the map.
                              We all within our boundaries
                              are only there politically
                              by habituation:
they traversed only natural boundaries followed the Platte
                                      flat heart of Territory..
              In the Traverse Theatre Edinburgh Pete Morgan showed me
              that the travesty is the idea of 'nation'
                              as geographically defined
              though we are Scots Nationalists of the mind
              and stand for some separation
                     because he shot as Scot, in words, and was heard
                     [their long drawn out Culloden Moor was for every poor
                     as a leader of idea.
              You have to have a people
```

                    [and the Cherokee had a language
          and an alphabet and were that
                              nearer all of us because of it]
          able to confer with age and check with youth
                                        for truth
          'we only have one wife because there is one moon
               nothing compares with that.'
Corpses now:
               'Relaxed post-mortem its not a smile
it means its time
          they should be underground'   that grin.
The freight-cars rock the railroad in its bed
                              the snake ululates from sleep
to sleep again after the weight
                    most plangent plainsmen since buffalo
lore persistent that the machine alone
                              will strike rhythms   'savages'
and we must follow them.
                    There are no laws in nature   assuages
                                        and the crew
grew up to three miles a day   long-meanders are 'Osages'
               this bus'day's mileage in three years
of laying-on buffalo trail
                    their migration road Cheyenne to Laramie
Union Pacific West
          even to laying on snow   their message was
                         we get up and go
in the night when the siren rolls and the air rattles after its vibrato
the same note on the tuning-fork steel Pullman Lackawanna Burlington
bison reverberate hoofs   backs like men   heavy forelocks
getting down to it   and making tracks
into territory   no puffs   near enough bluffs
bobbing country songs like corks   the wheels turn slow   pass
uproar   not asking   U.P.R.   and out of Nebraska   uprising.
                    There were no laws in Nature
          except that capital letter   direct for Washington.
                    In essays upon Domestication
          Darwin was biased against Indians   to all our education
                              in his estimation

                         the handsome Tierra-del-Fuegians
                were degenerate
Wallace*   who got to The Theory   first   but was less lucky
loved them   as a man he loved them
            like his theory his love was —not picked up by the media
                         and so forced into statement early
Wallace read Malthus and sensitively   made himself space
                  versed them permanently in his Diary
surprised to find so little competition in the race
                    [when population increases so does pressure]
in those days people didn't think of co-operation
                                    thought doom inevitable
for four years he didn't even put his thoughts to paper
                    [a restraint practically Indian]
in case
        his 'racial' ideas of evolution   [another word no one need have heard]

                         might prove 'shocking to the public.'
To Darwin they were not so tame as kine*   to be steered
            cowed-out   and so   they'll go
bison and indian   bones vertebrate our way.
          An old geyser or a box canyon   dead
          at the end of   the highway
              the old road north, the Dere Street
        of the Romans had their fort on the Rede River*
        Habitanicum
                its slopes square as Fort Read
                                  on the Plains
                      near water
        foursquare below the woodlined side
                              in quarters
          clear and open as putting-in-mind   their names
                what the Scots garrison has left behind
                         the mosstroopers*   7th Cavalry
        rievers* of the Scottish border
                         in their own order before America
        pele-towers* squared off against the raiders
                                  as along the Big Horn
        share-off the border situation

                                        look round for Rowan* and for thorn
                    the magic trees
                                    and find them lustier and shorn
like Ridsdale, West Woodburn, the road to Otterburn   no omen
                            in Northumberland today
                                        where there are soldiers still
            as over there you'll still hear gunshots on the air.
                After provocation, not mere   hinting   you will
Killingwell   two FBI men   kill   well
            for trespass with menaces [if you had your rights]
after a fair fight   circled off and rubbed out
            still concerned with killing well:
                                    their bodies swell
                a day or two*
                    out of blueing steady wind the red
            that head is
                and once again the land has bled
            as grassed lands seemed to   omen
                            with red poppies after the event
            they'll talk about as read
                            pass over on their poverty
            dismissing yours the way the wild man always wins
            away from fuss
                                            the frass
            instead has led
                        put it   down to   permanent grass
                for cows.

                            For the Indian
            the deadland badlands
                            but the tumbleweed's not dead
                its chittering   agin the
                                    windward head
                                        and there are seeds on the air
 being carried east and even
                        like pollen   why
in summer we attach ourselves to causes
foreign with that ration of unreason
                    and wandering is in the head

  we have only once to spend
        the end of feeling.   Yet
 'The Dakotas will come south with the buffalo
      they'll meet us brothers
        it was ever so.'*
  for all we interpreted their warring as competition
  on the grander scale of
        geology
        geography
        time
          life
         it was not so
  but cooperation, the cooperation thats coming in the anarchy
  we are onto now
      if we will stop and reconsider
  as Thunder, thunderbird over the plains they heard
      stopped to listen
         each moved into territory
  looked around
       the brown ground burned wet to green.
  Just enough to clear the view a bit, the clouds rolled on
  declining to lower land
       waiting their time to break
       don't ride cars to misunderstand
  to despise it out of hand
       stand in it
  its airs blow in us if we let them our breath and his
  not a destruction of the land like Caterpillar feet
          a building-up
  a land where people feel few.
       Thunderbird
  newcomer paleface. Beaten by blackfeet
  into black-meat survivor Brica MacGregor
  lived with the Blackfeet   overkill hunter
   back once he had tired of killing the animals
  he took his bagpipes with him
       for a quiet time

       the slowness with which everything happens
 their rhythm and it felt easy

                              and in time
reminding of a station wayside   way-wandering
                    in the Borders between England and Scotland
or of the little village school   at Lingdale [meaning heather-valley]
in North Yorkshire   after the death of its Iron Mining
                  Nature took over
                            the slowness with which
                                    life just gets paced out
                        round about.
                  No one to shout
                              the people parallel
                  they stand against their shacks and stare
not ignorant
                  but pipe-smoking so slow
                              you'll know   So
if you are ready we can go   to Jackson Hole
the innermost of the outer beyond   The Hole in the Wall
the way   being bent up and down
and all tourism in some wave form   from off a horse
or the freight cars run over you   lashing the land
a hundred beer and pop cans   now
and not one of them empty   there.
                              Poverty   Cheyenne
along your way, fifteen hundred miles   starvation
and caterpillars, grandfather-greybeard grubs *
                                          at the roots
of grasses   where in prostration your face is
listening to the singing of the wind over the miles, the rumble
in the earth.   We all come
                  to our Fort Robinson
as the Cheyenne   at the end of their tether   ours
   ours the wind on the grasses   to understand then   some
         defeated   undeflated
         insisting failure to them   but the best of them
for all its fetch of hundreds of miles
                        still walked on the wind   Shyela
                  it cut through them
In hospital delirium then
                  Killingbeck it was   [near Leeds]

          I dreamed of
digging-in at the killing pits* in North Yorkshire
to discover their true nature
                      found they were iron mines only   once
in Lingdale and Leeds they play, the childrens street game
                    'Cowardy Cowardy Custer'
Compare their songs today outside the Pine Ridge School   today.

        Crazy Automobile   he died of steel
                'when it was still good   to live'.
     Time was, they took the white man in   hospitality
      especially if he   like me   was what we call crazy
            like   Captain Humberstone Lyon
ex-Waterloo, where he'd had two muskets
we would say he'd got both barrels
at Rendezvous   the Mountain-Men's annual gathering of the clans
      had   for the record   his private painter with him
an occasional poet
       later known as 'drunkard' to Custer
                the big man along the Powder River
    teetotaller before the term was struck   there
    made up his mind about the campaign, and drunk
      with Sheridan   ['only good Indian … dead']
           to the end
                there were then 4000 Cheyenne
    in Washeta villages before the election issue
    which tipped the scales in Custer's direction: he expected
to be able to turn the Sioux back from them   on the
              Little   Big   Horn.
   Life in the grass is   seed heavy with its message
    to us clear   full of bones   as we walk it
the wire   any wire does the same
    a country built once of feeling things
                  the telegraph?   Sand land, again
  in bed alone, but coming to,   wind-land
  running in cuttings like the eternal train
           the noise insistent again across the plain
      its grain   lines run down about a century

                    [no-one goes by train in the Dakotas now
                                                    old pick-ups prowl
            the rocks which are   loaded with fossil fish of all knowledge
            no new species every half-mile even   as in the redbeds* of Scotland:
this is a stretched out land
                                            where nothing stands
            unswaying   except   the Black Hills   at
            the corner of the eye   unreal   corneal   sore
                        with the wind in it
travelling a destruction of brutality by vigor or sensitivity
or sensuality   by rigor.
                They talk of   loaded brutes*
                    'Only cargo acceptable is twenty loaded brutes'
            by   oilpipelines miles
broken-down   to mustang
                                        musty warning   Indian
        [by smell, its music]   mustered
                        must assemble
                            red-beds like Cromarty in Scotland
            full of fossils   life extinguished
is not life eroded.
                    The dinosaurs remain bone by bone
the plants they browsed on   stain by stain
                        their own their own
the life in the grass is the shape you see, eyes pressed
closed tight:
            light like the yellow movement in the cuckoo-spit*
    the most fragile life
                you can't hunt and be half-hunter.
'We are free in our poverty'
                    While men are born to prison
in themselves
                'that's why no one cares whatever Indians do.'
                        I never met
anyone not affected by the Black Hills, one way or other
something   like Ireland
            to sing about out of the land   not tinned   entirely
or   that tune recycled in the Alex-Johnson reception area   [Rapid City]
    in sight   MarIon Brando   debarred   insistent   to be   inside

Edward Drinker Cope [no drinker] and   O. C. Marsh   palaeontologists
fought it out here over bones
                                like you could go into a bar so
soundlessly   running in tune   America: all one tune
and they'd take it up   possessively   the people
here on vacation.
                              And one or two,
after melancholy and not blues but seeing only broken hills
where every footfall's faithful to itself
                                as it is in grass
               of who might pass
Lincoln's Western Union Omaha to Salt-Lake by Pawnee Country
                    Some of the navvies, shockers
                                        Morse-tapped like Harley-Davidson
overhead-valve-rockers
                          Sinking Wells   and Sage
       Spotted Horse   Ogallala.
                     To pass and leave no trace
wild white goat
the nasty old man of the hill country.   In his old white coat
a greater enemy than Custer this protoscientific muster
                                      anthropologists
the equivalent of Sibley who, above the law,
to classify The Birds at Yale's Peabody Museum
imported the important birds eggs from sixty-four countries
and a hundred and sixty-four collectors only twelve of them with licences
                         illegality
                                under the Lacey Act
oh yes he was eventually [after the captains had brought in
        the most expensive evidence of his sin]
                      fined three thousand dollars for it.
           Justice
      'democracy is a white man being a white man
    not   letting an Indian walk where he will'
                                Shot at Pine Ridge by the F.B.I.
   Two fall guys   like twin fallpipes
     propped at the side of the house   meanwhile
'You cannot call it scenery that is too small a word'
applied to things comprehensible to eye and brain as of heard

```
                familiar things like pastures and horizons
                                      to things subject to measure
                          'only the smallest flower is treasure'
on the ridge, not quite bare                            so
                    you could see porcupines had been there
recently
             clean aspen bone      split light stem         bole
condensing the Open Range finding         actual artifice     first-glance
                          in idea advance
knowing what it is split off for you            when you find it
                                                    meaning is not whole
timber
         the cling of country
                          and weather saying no.          You know
it doesnt take just courage to go out in it
              it takes              the effrontery to country
that Indian isnt.         The courage may be there
but you dont still just want to go out
                it isnt necessary
to watching assimilating        drawing leads
                                      just be wary
the stranger before he's in has all eyes on him
it is the best way to be sure                  to get to know
                    mountains in the distance aren't going
          anywhere
                     and they're as good for that
the light gives them expression          'and you know that
          your writers at least    look to the hills
                          even the missionaries say that'
          'The Gods are in the Black Hills'
                          the youth, his arms akimbo on the ridge
             Bear Butte*
waits for his word for life
                          fasts
          the insistent noise of traffic    overscores of miles recorded
          in the grasses        echoes            running east
          all one beast
             down the steps of the land      hand in hand
                high plains
```

                    great plains
                         lakes plains
                                   hardly any prairie.
Oh no on parallel lines we run   on
to Doncaster* or Fort Laramie
sleeping down to London or up to Butte
we'd pull up beside the sign   creak-rails   the sentiment
LOAD LIMITED TO ONE LOADED BRUTE   [at at time]
          sediment of sum butte mesa his cave means
   the media are in the stars. We wait for signs
and watch the water-rail*   on migration
lost, walk the plank   of   this rail-station
            threshold   and we turned over
                              mugged by the rails   I was
by Nez Percé   once
          cleaned out in Edinburgh
by a skirt that led by the red rocks of the Jed
restored from such greed by the people of the Rede
and the family of Hugh MacDiarmid
                ['Red as they come']
hospitality   the slap of the parritch-pat
on porridge
        the small house   'all thats needed
                          near at hand'   And, like rebuilt Fort Kearny
at Ridsdale
        the biggest pele-tower   isnt it   in ruin
                          burned day and night
1839 to 1878 and then the rest of Britain caught up with it
                economic sag
you know it by its slag
this the steam engine house of some smelter
fancy building industrial on the old pele lines!
it doesnt do   it disturbs the dust of minds
preferring to think   in categories
fixed
local ironstone always was low grade
                                'the best
pipestone was Superior'   thousands of miles of trade
brought it out west with stories to light evenings in it

                'in such country expose yourself to your initiation'
            like here we tell them at Joe's place, Rapid City
       gray block utterly   unlovely   I want to spend ages
          stages in the sun as you do until you knew watching waiting hills
          that see   usuage continue   continuity   instead
              unsteady   I drive hard for the Indian where I
              can get to know him   beheaded

                             ahead of the media   Indian dignity
              you simply have to be
                           as they were when they killed the FBI men
              essentially
                        the FBI trespassed
                                       on the Bad Land
          all that was left of hunting-grounds, handed over
                                                             'after treaty eaten.'
              Its corrugations as we passed over to Philip, South Dakota   pink
          tinged
                                        the wrinkled cringed
              a little   caroused   their rousing Pine Ridge   felt the pulse
                                  merry in adversity
              the peas rattled on the wind
                                 with children of all ages in one classroom
just as it had been the underprivileged village school in England's old iron district:
              Lingdale   not staring into starry boredom
with more stuff shirts out on vacation
but   too poor to be numbered with them   and for no other reason
in the mercy of the land   no smother
                    and no other
              'Why
                    you cant retreat   further west   you see
              there's Wyoming   why
                           where
                           you can see
                           further than and less
                           than anywhere else on earth'
                                                  higher
                                  and more broken   the Tetons Range
its raw teeth set on edge by wire

                              enclosed as is desire
by it   so you
                    set that flywheel turning in the sky
the blue gray grows to
                        when the thunderstorm is by
    and it rubs out the sun and starts to fly
    its own hawks thunderbolts
                      and you have to try
          to listen, watch the rock face grass and see why
the faces of living-stone sphinx* until as from the chrysalis
the originals will come full circle as the winds knit the storm
its blackness over   the faces are not Indian
they'll fret under frost, they'll not keep warm
toys for our souls when the tribes run tribal again
                                        until then
cut and fit new images if they will work and last.
                                    Bare Bear Butte
        surrounded by a round wall of sound   and wind
        as a medieval city   and as skinned
        skilled leather workers hide the souls under
                        as empty of first resources and as filled
        the people will still look to it: you cant take such hills away
                    like one man wanted to 'To Florida'
at the Trailways depot, Cody, and the bar in Sheridan
                        he told me.   Looking on
the seer rests on the words and will not say
                        until you've formed
the words for him yourself
                  too much today
                                is being asked immediate
of the Indian   forcing him   to that false position
that doesn't take into the consideration   stars   land
and the rest of creation.
                        And we got up to go
                    and I
        not with the Florida florid
                    or the girl opening her blouse.
        To the Mountain   more massive than the tandem
            steam or diesel   used over the Great Plains

            and moving like it, in the wind   we made of
flanks heaving heavy cloud   across the continental divide
                        motionless or travelling every one of them
a herd of buffalo in original emotion   motivation   dung
their motive power
                    electrophysical the backdrop is
            moving electrically as any engine
                        power
the smoke more folk make   oblate
      noises perfume night
            like any mother's rivers further South
the quivers   about a continent's   broad mouth
                            of teeth
of alcohol   wood   alcohol   inchoate   incontinent
                            grumbling freight
stars ablaze over   the little stars   it makes
                      like thunder
          and us under
                thunderstorm again
local as a man's hand in such a land
a pressing down upon the Indians head   eye turned
no newcomer more weasel-eyed against the light
              the lurking devil in the Aaron Copland ballet.
                                                  Set
against such continual pushing   continual punishment
                  and the only parchment   mattering
is the skin after the wind or in the dryness meant   muttering
to the ground its cracking up
              full of bones, revealing them, after the duster
      a muster
            after Custer
                the Dinosaur Rush
                      Marsh
Mudge   Carney   Douglas   Homes   and Edward   Drinker   Cope
of cluttered study
          like more Anthropology   but more down to earth
between   them Cope and Marsh named new to science all of
136 new species
       ['The Indians decimated in population faster']

             and they had their chronicles down the years
in Indian memory and the watercolors of Arthur Lake
and photographs in sepia of seam-faced   Curtis   Indians.
                                                                After the rains
a bone cabin   O.C. Marsh made of them
                                          dinosaurs and trains
and Indians   all   'Dead as the Dodo.'
washed out hearts and brains.

Glossary and Notes to *Rushmore Inhabitation*

* The Thunderbird of American Indian myth has been personalised, by this naturalist, as the eagle. (Page 113)
* Alfred Russell Wallace, contemporaneously with, but independently of, Charles Darwin the originator of the classic Theory of Evolution. (Page 115)
* Kine: North British term for cattle. (Page 115)
* The route of Roman subjugation of the Celtic tribes of North Britain. The Rede River runs south from the present border in the Cheviot of Northumberland. (Page 115)
* Moss-troopers: Scots or English border marauders, a term more or less synonymous with Rievers: Their allegiances varied. (Page 115)
* Pele-towers: Fortified house or church size stone buildings. (Page 115)
* Rowan Trees: [Mountain Ash] for the warding-off of evil; no Great Plains equivalent. (Page 116)
* The affair of June 26 1975 when on the day that 133,000 acres of Dakota reservation were [apparently without the full consent of the tribes] transferred to U.S. Park & Recreation Department. Two F.B.I. men and one Indian were killed in a shoot-out elsewhere on the Pine Ridge Reservation. (Page 116)
* Cheyenne motto. (Page 117)
* Grandfather Graybeard Grubs [North America]: Daddy Long legs grubs or Leather Jackets in England. (Page 118)
* Killingbeck and Killing Pits: English place-names of uncertain etymology, but suggestive. (Page 119)
* The Redbeds of Cromarty: Where Hugh Miller pioneered as Cope and Marsh did in the West. (Page 120)
* Brutes: A unit of railway load. (Page 120)
* Cuckoo-spit: Abundant in the grasslands of both North America and Europe, a frothy material clinging to grassblades and sheltering small insects [*Hemiptera*, fragile plant bugs]. (Page 120)
* Bear Butte: The place of Indian waiting-on for the spirit guidance, near the Black Hills. (Page 122)
* Water-Rail: Similar to the Virginia Rail, [*Rallus limicola*]. The European Water Rail is a great wanderer on migration. (Page 123)
* Sphinx of the Egyptian desert, a representation more subtle than those of American presidents at Mount Rushmore in the Black Hills. Also, in nature, the hawk-moth family whose large pupae or chrysalises keep their own vigil until their season. (Page 125)

The Compression of the Bones of Crazy Horse

(Wahtunka Witko) Oglala Sioux, 1842–77, leaving no known likeness no known resting place.   Translated words, spoiled, bracketed, are his own and others' of The People

> **PLEASE DON'T
> DISTURB WILDLIFE:**
> Ingleby Estates

Moor Grouse for the Big guns.
                       As the Cleveland Blackamore Hills do for North Yorkshire
so the Black Hills presentiment the westward mountains eastward
Blue Clouds piled loud as Harney's Peak
spilled dark on their pediments
                                         impediments to Ultimate Destiny
    the heart-rest of Plains Indians extend
                            the West eastward biogeographically
withstand   resistance to
        the cars
a Horned Lark bare-place *Eremophila alpestris* rings
the whole hemisphere   only his decreasing circle sings   day-stars
(I am of one mind
with the place I am)   single syllables span
the broad dome, the Red 'Valley' girdle inset around it in trance
geomorphologists naming it the Race Track, Red Cinders
Sundance to Rapid City to Hot Springs and back north to Sundance
from the laccolithic ancient centre outward   granitic, igneous
indigenous as its Indian, like them a Quaternary Development
crystalline   schistose metamorphic
                                                         like its people
unglaciated   limestone-plateau   sedimentary
        parkland on this
the whole ringed by the Dakota Coteau and Hog-back
              (if I were a rock I would he very old
              and lie around all day)*
cheek by jowl with the Bad Land   this rich heartland
      the hearth of the sky's teepee
              (I am close to the Holy Hills   and will always see
      how happy
      the mule-deer will be   picking-up new scents:

              they are like me and will hide me)

    the bones of the land   scapula   and sacrum
        the comic and the leader in his body is the mime

> BLACK HILLS HIDEAWAYS
>   (REAL ESTATE)   starkshirtsplitskirts

tourist twist eyes West tint windshields
              feel the rhythm of the concrete rafts
will not get out of the car much   under the sky   riding
the arc of air   the anvil-cloud in tension like a coracle
Sans Arc   they lined-up   Minneconjou
           skull and clavicle of a mink pulled out of river
        Till between England and Scotland, 1976
Cheyenne, Brulé, Santée   Yankstoné
      Northumberland umbral understalks talk
     along the Greasy Grass, the Little-Big Horn 1876
Blackfoot Sioux, Oglala, Hunkpapa   closed the circle
a few Arapaho, Grosventres.   Custer Died For Your Sins
the whole bow of that village bent in tension and the grass spins
    Sprague's Pipit the only endemic   characteristic
diagnostic of the High Plains   signs sings, spring in winter
(the winter is so wide, it fills the skies
does it reach your heart?)*   In the Pine Ridge Schoolroom
Chungkpi Opi Wahkpala — The Creek Called Wounded Knee
Big Foot Dead In the Snow With His Band and The End of Those Wars, 1890
warmth-being-what you bring into the morning   pipits warning
      'sing-a-sting-a-stinging-sing'
towering, flushed out of short grass on the Hogback
                   hard-to-see

tingling to listen to
(The War Was For
The Black Hills)
              territory being all twisted up
            by metamorphosis
          like this schist is
     so that the lines in it cannot be recognised
       they have been so separated

                                                'I will lead them up and down
                                            break their legs in the prairie-dog town
                                             I will lead them up and down'
High-Plains inflection   the most elementary discipline-diction
A lonely tree speaks to an old telephone-pole   it says
'The snow has made me cold and weary
But that's what winter is'   And the telephone-pole answers
'Some more is on its way')

on being released
the captive raptor
turns its claws on itself
and its own kind   subtended, displaced
not a wild thing any more!   bear no relation to the ground they are from
                                  the poorest land: the Reservation
                                       waits and had been waiting
                                    clear for the cleaning of the land

                                              Waiting for Blue Grama Grass
                                                  Butelova gracilis
                                              and Buffalo Grass *Buchloé*

   | EXIT FOR FAUNA PARK ... SAUNA |

In Custer National Park today the apparently-wild animals play
blue skirted locust *Dissoteira*, fluttering Common Wood-nymphs and Satyrs
their apparently-idyllic, apparently-alpine way   and the British in Arabia sprayed
their locusts and the sheep lost wool and died   you know

   | U.S. SPRAYS | whole States | AGAINST RODENTS | and Gooks
                                                           Allah and Manitto
keep as-careful books.
                    And whatever happened to the Predator
when English banks closed-off the Open Range   before 1910
and the Indian   with bringing-them-in   to the Agencies
                          Ironically for an arid land
Bad Land Topography has developed a Fine-Drainage Texture ...
in one of these Beheaded Streams in Blind Valleys
the bayonetted heart and bones of Crazy Horse are buried
                                          in White River Sands

with the carocoids of dinosaurs his coracle is clavicled
                                          one grave that will not be robbed.
After The Winter They Didnt Come In   Crazy Horse's choice
when Little Big Man who had fought in the snow with him became a Police-man
reminds me of the subtlety those Americans come to England or Europe to find
they've left behind   (Land is not on paper.
How can we sell what we walk upon)   The State Experts
they thought *Mustela nigripes* was gone forever (Pispiza etopta sapa:
The Black-footed Ferret   just because they had not seen it
If a Wasichu looks at you with malice —   you will chew
his gut, hypnotise him to   bad luck   just as they do
the Prairie-Dog *Cynomys)*   (never mind Old Nokomis)
there's gold in them thar   someone's Going To Get It
Where did the Buffalo go

       for a while birches lash each others' faces
       fray in the wind, strip leaves
       and then the wind changes
       and aspens take up the fray and chant
       braes brant aslant   the sperrit it is a widderin' thing
                                                         like the willow-tree wind in a quiet wood
                                                       Or this circumscribed cottonwood's skullridge
                                        Whistling to us   of an arrow struck on wood

it shakes confined in a radius   rings sharp   marks out a chord
sharp syntax   awed, stood   (we stuck to the land, quivered with it
As I ride through by B.M.W. and H-D   Cheyenne to Laramie   the old buffalo-trail
erosion pavement you can see thru   a peneplain or a Wayland's etch-plain
(the ambush I am in charge of   because for me it is)   I conspire with geography
(geology is under) like the Pronghorn Antelope walking this Gangplank over the High Plains
where they've laid their rails on the pedeplain the buffalo made for them
(Earth doesn't belong to anyone, but we are all part of it)
                                              struggle only ever made warriors
or poets
'Texas' or 'Dakota' means 'our people'
                                 to come here
                                                 I will ask the Dakotas their permission

RIDERS BEWARE GOPHER-HOLES

```
to the Prairie-Dog Town the Burrowing Owl            Speotyto cunicularia
brings consternation                         there's always life in a lower level
              specularisation
                         sun motes
                              to relaxing of concentration
                         walking or riding I have felt some tension
a surprise
       sudden through the legs with a stiffness in the thighs
             unrelated to any extra exercise
                                             a suspension
the dregs of consciousness then
                       the drifting-off into a dream
like the twitch that comes on sudden    near-to-sleep
                              in a sinking-soft sense of stream
with surprise remembered after years
                              those seeming-same sensations
reverse the accepted screen of given appropriations
approximations                    the same extension
                                  between the eyes
                    as I passed them, Herb Elliot and Frank Shorter
the glint of whitened quartz-sand glimpsed bleached boreally
                              High Plains and North Yorkshire
the limn of the White River Sands reaches back shear of gyration
so the distant horse dance before the eyes    their legs foreshortened
no mirage                               your quarter-horses. Crazy Horse
and your reported dream.

                 That stiffness in the thighs, long-distance eyes
                    with the vision in, on stream
                  is the Mixture As Before
                for Jimmy Deans - Moves - Camp     a century later
            who   only dreamed of quality      with Equus        equality
```

                              He was forever out on his own
                    no matter   like El'Aurens
                into the deserted space his place the pace of it   nomad
                              c.f. Pamir
Hi-Ho'ing   Kill-deer *Charadrius vociferus*
the Long Gun of the hunter and the long-drawn querulous call   so that they all,
the tourists, think our Lapwing Plover must be a Bird of Prey
it's no more that than, say, their
                              Western Meadowlark *Sturnella neglecta*
                                                            forgotten
by the rancher as the Indian   'just something that was there'
to sing in the spring, describe a circle   limited, in the air
                (Earth Doesn't Belong to Anyone, But We Are Part Of It)*
(the snow flakes are talking too   they say
Our Friends are on their way)*
when you'd have thought it needed most
it's out there on its own.

| DIVIDED HIGHWAY | The Winter They Didn't Come In
he had to get rid of his friends
                          to bring out his tactics   make them
work over and above his love   that is his measure.
Now the Promoters 'of the wilderness' are
                'ordering the mess', out of greediness.
Forget the rhyme and we can begin to see rhythm
being is a place for hunting, standing out it
                                    the Black Hills will be again
the Sun and its Dance, again
                      national sovereignty somewhere in this is
there is no absentee-landlordship of the spirit
                          The security of sun had dancing made
motes in it are Sprague's Pipits   retina'd
                as green the Prairie Rattlesnake *Crotalus viridis*
just suppose it is as it is   for a moment
            The Black Hills and the Bad lands are juxtaposed
(the one is beside the other as sister and brother)
        positive magic and negative desert in aspect

       black-full with pine or yellow with empty light.
(I have asked the Lakota, expect their permission to fight)

at Wounded Knee battlefield, April 1973

*Contributions from schoolchildren, Pine Ridge 1973.

The boxed words are:
1. a noticeboard on the North Yorkshire Moors, The 'Blackamore' of their best authors
2. & 3. sign beside I 90, S. Dakota
4. U.S. National Park sign
5. Road Sign, Wounded Knee, April 1973

Shorter Poems

The Thieves' Road

Of pollution and Missouri dams limn the east
Blackhills cloud on the West, the black sill(s)
Over this land, where an East and a West
meet in flora and fauna, and is Lakota
hovers more than the cloud that presages
storm in its billowing up over the veldt
follows a greeting, the raven of thingvellir
in its chasm that shows/falls in to the earth's centre
splitting along the meeting of elements, felt
      They brought the tree in, made a maypole:
      were the dances of Merrymount so different
      from the witch parties of rival Salem?
Failing the earth – but why the American
flails in greed/dearth of spirit-feeling for the land
if a man gets away with stealing he is dead
if a people … they will have lost their head
and killing eagles is no worse than the sand
that blows after they've killed off prairie-dog

Overhead of Yellowstone breaks the thunder
magma-chamber Yellowstone quarter under

1872 the Yellowstone National Park
still the Indians' hunting ground in part
their living/livelihood and sacred-ground too good
for them – not least Chief Joseph would
pass through; Nez Percé trail of blood

1874-7 the great grasshopper (locust) invasion,
as if on the Indians' side …

The High Plains People died with the Prairie
'Grasshoppers'/ locusts

Coming Home Off The Hills, Urra

MacDiarmid was right; it is a wonder any worth survives the massive pox
and the denial of dreams   like after
[after fourteen pints of Theakston's   remembered
Busby Stoop to Sproxton Best Bitter beer by the Fox.]
The tallest man I ever saw was a highway-patrolman Niobrara way
long easygoing nature he had the shortest hair and the shortest
long consideration thong chewed-baccy thing to say
so mebbe its thank God for ther tranparency mekkin a wunda sum
"a wonder anything of worth" will 'Come *sensitively* today...

survives' *yen*
an
Jim Ryun   'n Billy Mills
(who was   the other wun)
because they run   and run-
collishun   jus glancin offen the bum
o' the policeman (that's the Reservation one)
rednecks wither big gun jackets on
ther clothes themselves to brutal, stun.

the poor-white   beaten on the bus
came to us beaten-up, one of us
had sign language
Naive pronounce sentence if able:
Native Siouian slur the terminal syllable
sense of guilt dumbs.
            titon wan
     you can face back upon
The People All One

Feb. 28, 1977 (The centenary of a signing-away of the Black Hills)

revised 1990, 2005

Rocky Mountain Locust Strewn

At the Araphaho wedding something stirred
and lifted real and artificial buckskin dresses
the inches the slew wind   suctions grasses
an intake of breath of Iyan Kara – great Scott
Momaday rings in the ears a rush that way
                            in their excesses
rising above the risings, for their part
                (Bobwhites?) quails
and meadow larks more akin to distant starlings
nowadays – they'd not arrived in His Day
nor the prairie 'English' skylark – my start –
in to discovery of such unexpectedness
                day and night, none to a lot
until the mountain(s) and until the prairie fails

                        as long as the grasses grow
the winds blow   and the (other) waters flow
they come unbidden from somewhere hidden, they go
with/wherever untaught thoughts forever strew

                      storms can be becoming
                      from nothing, sudden
                            and anywhere

              Sundance Fasting
              self-mutilation   Preparation
              Commitment to AN ACT (to come
                      ITSELF AN ACT
           CAN I DO WHAT I 'HAVE TO' DO?
           WHAT HAS TO BE DONE

April in 1622, High Plains

Down quite cloud dawn foot high white grey thaw-hunt while-wind white off the
Knowing-not Crow slow fingers single deep hoofmarks ice melt-soft turf
softer than dew

Cropp-marks more punctuated than that the bison had at gramma-grass
different from antelope rhythm rippled out from worked little
all is in circles; this must be worthy and wary, standing-circles

Knowing Arapaho to turn (out of) the wind before (numb) nostrils burn raw
wind constant, way-constant, different
wet at the new awareness

Get hold those first few rolled-round fewmets whole met alive still warmth
to come of their mould

in fungi toed earth dew-blacked about their turned-spheres the nose new dressed processed
toadstool crop of old

pulling fur-soft pair from between the untorn spur tendrils of a single-nod Shyela bedstraw
this is where the horse had evolved, after all!

lay in the hand a newland as deerslot-soil contemplate pattern-relating
space new   foil to the heart pace   to oil all the trail
steady to where the herd at shelter stirred lick the sick foal
already the same Arikari   still jealousy centuries old in 1972
tense as Cheyenne eyeshining   finds Indigene-divining; horse-hole-to-hole wild
from out of nowhere

Out of Spanish out of tarpan Asian first tentative Teton-eat-Horse to Have Borne
neither stirrup nor spur. For

The People. It seemed fresh enough to have bee dropped the Day Before

'Allied Extermination'

(A sign on the San Jacinto road
about twenty miles north of Houston:
in other words, not Madison Avenue)
Animals and Indians have been failures
to extirpate since old Charles Darwin.

They calculated that the Prairie Dog
a charming social rodent, nonetheless ate,
thirty-two of them, what a single hog
or half a cow would. So they poisoned an entire state.

'I do not live in the rocks, safe places,
nor even in the high trees, where grace is:
I built my lodges on the plains earth'.

'I would be to each of you just the same
to pass by, not noticing if I'm lame:
another summer fox come out of his thicket'.

'Feel me, for wind is not better than breath
and any way found past the living is wicked.'

Crossing Minnesota, West

>Come west for the rhythms of the Going

it gets slower, with a pardon-me at every intersection
and roadside signs in Old-Norse, so that you know
the trees have to he planted, and they are Russian olives
and the Nazis reinforced this land after Concentration
and their synagogues are all that is agog, the rest is slow

'them slows all dried-up, haven't seen any rain at all'
'a few birds, but nothing like there used to be' you know
Kandiyoh Farmers Union silos stand on undistilled land
the cider is unfermented, rail and road cling for Company
otherwise the country plants 'touch-me-not' in Mennonite hats

until, the lakes; Atwata, Sheerwater, Minnetonka, Stillwater
Grasmere has come-on here: Green Lakes staked matrons pantheist
exist on imported Fiord Water, Whisky, while *Ranatra lineata*
deliberately as in Europe measures out in Power lines
U.S. 12's concrete rafts' asphalt seams continues and combines

Grove City. Willmar, Cosmos, Tapestry and Diamond
by their water-towers we shall know them, by their shorthand
geometry has come to telegraph top-ties patterning
the old Indian signal
Picasso's breadrolls at the table
Grain-Belt gives artists' hands

'Blue-blooded' *for Ed Dorn*

Farms died; but, always going-forward
working the mines and Smith's Dockyard
my grandfather and his Clarence cricket-crew
(rolling-mills spin-bowler, blastfurnacemen
close-fielders); men of all skills and all parts …
Great-grandfather, and my grandmother there too
gave one hundred percent, made sure I do –
(not *like* I do, but at least they knew
I'd to do what was for me to find to do)

T'other grandfather half-Piegan; that's half-Bloods
with relations among Arapaho, Teton-Sioux
laughing "you can *tell*, when his blood was up"!
harm, and true; but not first thing in the morning
warned with Black-Wasichus' "Ah'm Black and Blue"
warmed to their work when they had *wanted* it,
hunted but not beyond plenty, 'Spirit-Granted'…
yawned *with* the Bull Elk, not shooting at it
"too smooth a morning", but punned being 'jerky' about it ….

Dec 30th 1990/ 1st Jan 1991
Montana/South Dakota
The Ride

There is not difference, we are all offence
here in the open light, as I have done
under their caresses, into their dark essence
put your head in these prairie grasses
sweet as those used in the sweat lodge
up from their most complex rootstocks
sod not for the plough. The Beloved of God
is kept for incense and insects and all earth
the bountiful, the faithful, the sun's wife
the partner and mother of every man
not even the farmer can lay sole claim on:
whatever the greed, the politics, the strife.
You do not sell the land you walk upon
but murdered Crazy Horse with a knife*

* 'longknife' (bayonet)

Gray Alders

You distinguish these from our
streamside alders, flood-plain markers
by their gray hairs.
                              These are
sagamores of trees, old and proud,
once the totems of the Delawares
following the fall line rivers to the Atlantic.
Their pollen goes over the earth like the Lenape did

                        In this English garden
you can see alders are close to birches
in federations of seeds and of bloods
with the woodland Indians
before Sheffield secateurs and tomahawks.

1969

Storm Crossing Texas

impermeabilities wait
      sleep-time   lightening up
                              sunburst blues
keeping turkey-buzzards down
                            the storm within
PERMIAN BASIN   an oil-well town
the only place the bus pulled off to drink down
a hundred gallons in acknowledgement
                            while
                     Scissor-tailed Wagtails
ignored HAPPINESS IS EXPANDING grooming tail-feathers
their boards groaned in brown wind
GENERAL CONSTRUCTION   nests   Thor Big Daddy
overheard signalled intentions
bent his finger to the dust   BRONCHO CHEVROLET
out of the skillet north and rising
blotting up JACKSON THE KING PRAWN BROKER and
HARLEY-DAVIDSON into the Panhandle

1967

for Paul War Cloud, a Lakota artist, 1971

'Giving is everything', but only a hint
like the dry creekbeds in the Badlands:
"Wakanbonesands"!, giving me the print.
He listens to my poetry, eyes closed tight
to the wind, and taps 'Ghost' rhythm night
meadowlarks days will say say nothing
but through me. A way to everything –
a spire to art by plain statement –
striving for the apparent, bluntness
representational, and by that 'very' likeness
stately, stating it is not art, nor artless;
a principle of nature is vagueness;
a principle which seems to panic most men
but it does not panic the 'Indian'
he is not for 'our' haste, selfishness/legality 'precision'
though most particular as to his responses to nature
and what we patronise as his rituals
and disregard as maybe 'primitive' religion
he worked out over centuries of experience
of nature we have not known; or forgotten.
We laugh at the 'uncertainty' even of Gauguin
the 'childishness' of Momaday or Longfellow
because we have not seen, and do not know.
What is most obvious in natural-history
is its nature; 'vagueness', its internal force
requires our 'investigation', acknowledgement, of course.
Sense the intangible dream, the apparent blonde
hence conviction – there *is* a life beyond
prepared for us 'fasting for the vision' …
just as colour is vibration
just as is light, and voice, and sound
the rocks themselves, "which alone stay around"*
War Cloud he wanted to be buried above ground
life and art not for preaching a 'message'
but for their insights' pulsations' *massage* …

[Wind River Reservation, 1975, revised 2004.
*from a child's poem in my class at Pine Ridge 1973/4]

Bear Skull   for a third edition

When has the nature of a bear meant sulks?
From worn-down teeth we've found, husks
jaw wider ridged than this escarpment's
limestone reflected in his enamel cusps;
no top soil in a cave but stalagmitic cave-earth.
Hunter you spoke of as following-up,
found another in the cave, and waiting there
"An thet wun, aint had nuthin done to 'm yit"
the whole animus hard to break down –
the rest of the bear is nowhere, in the air?
Yet so fragile we broke his paper thin vault
for all our nervous, careful excavation
Richard in Teesdale, nineteen sixty-seven
bearteeth necklet, but wolf skull the crown!

Whiskery darkness flickers bearclaws
but wolf breath; darkness feels scars
arcs the claws blunted intil; provisional
less ephemeral than the quarrymens', cavers',
but still incertae sedis having nothing
of the organic or of the provenance
unless that one bone needle registers
other than rivals for one living-space;
curves might persist, cave bears have to be faced.
So that the *polar* bear skull in another cave
high in the Northwest far from arctic coasts
leaves even more space for vital organs missing
and questions. We asked; what great spirit gave
wolves, bears, and you and me, to boast?

(For Richard Thompson, Teesdale Cave)
Forest-in-Teesdale & Washington State
1967, 1980, rev. 2004

Snake turns through the great trench of West Wyoming

The serrations along horizons wind a film frame by frame forward.
From off this bluff we watch the moose far below in the bottom
before I realise this was *the* viewpoint – look he's up to his hocks
in the marsh, and lifts his head to bellow similarly arrived at –
for Angel Adam's photographic portrait of this same scene
and with similar clouds atop the peaks yonder they were made positive
bellow we cannot hear for distance, print we cannot remember for the life of us
three great sloughs, levelled series of terraces, stand back
from the present river's course below, as if in deference
as the Snake has lowered herself in stages in the presence
of meanders; hardly obsequiousness, much less taken-aback
 but respect of magnificence between the great ranges –
the contrasting ranges of the great breastpeaks, Tetons
to the west; and the Grosventres, the Big-Bellies, to the east

Behind the obscuring wall which throws its pall with sunset
over the buttes she distinguishes, moon comes up as sudden
progressing even to your face as the sun had recently left it
its shadows raced like antelope over the flats to find us.
The omen the answering call of elk we had not heard the rivals
though they are near, and abundant, you (also) say "co-eval"
sharing surely some of the sensation of these stars growing
over us all until not merely pinpricks but some are glowing
and some are coals and some diamond points and focus
is harder for their abundance. The scarcity of thought
under such a show, the slowness of the awareness (of it)
whatever it is or whatever we call it which silences us
but not the elk, and, no nearer but for the thinner air
the moose braying challenges more than his fellows there

(the snake river runs to slake all my thirsts aches)

Fasting, to the Arapaho Sundance, 1998

What it is makes us declares us
as one species, the same Peoples:
the round of the sky, itself no god
the round of the earth, forever a sod
for to break it is to hurt the mother
as it is to dam up/the round of water
made for us by the round of hills
their same round the round of our times
the holy man's round of reason fills
as nearly as the round seasons' rimes
tipis and their great circles to share
round the pole that is sacred bare
rare as it can come round once a year
wakan makes/dares us only to declare

Vermilion from Standing Rock somewhere
Ochre baked on oak coals and, cold-
pounded to powder; the only gold
(the other maddens men and nation)
Minnesota blue needing no preparation
from where the thousand lakes cast sky down
when it is clear; near the Falls of Minnehaha
white from White Clay county, South Dakota
Black from dead stars mixed in bison fat
we are of what we make again for that
found-Kiyipi in the Prairie Dog town
The only red to stay is from burnt clay
blood of the dead but running this/that day
we are what we put on, cut off, bleed away!

Thinking Put in Mind of Kerouac

'alright if this Indian Summer holds'
                                            mind a long way from the present
                 'but what does that hound-dog think he's doing'
who is he trying to convince   and what is assent?
                  we have a fraction of this consciousness
             eeoo   eoo   eoo   Now please don't misconstrue.
No yaps   soprano accent   then tremulous crescendo
a trailing back   slack enough to have taken our scent
this isn't malice   but there is a moon   ascendant
          war   wur   eeeooo 'un   man-if-you-have-a-gun
there's nothing in my song but hopefulness
                            and it is being sung
for everyone in sound that's you and me, Wyoming,
                           up an ascent.

                the bivouac's less cosy
                           the door
cannot be closed. The silence grows
                      not like after a baby's crying
just letting the ears hear grass and the sky lightening at last

Opening McClure   a while away I heard her say
(Jack) you have to be some singer.   I heard you in the night …

                                 (KYOTE)

At Pine Ridge 1973

Coyote calls from my foxhole
shy for others to pause on patrol
sky with no faceless officialdom
and the faces from which they come

unrelaxed, but they are my brothers
who had none, even if unseen
men and enemy 'friends' are one
kola' we call all, whatever message ...

to remember a battle a man
must, even a long-range one
have been taught dc-briefing rigid
and what is not a matter of recall

the man must be back in his body
and that body just exactly then,
not 'memory', which is hackwork
which you can elaborate or shirk

because it is not organic, whole
as the midnight sleeping shout is
innocence must not be lost at all
nor the clout that led to rout

fear is controlled by its details
as anything else can be handled
any phenomena in outer nature

The badger-holes are there, so
where, then, are the badgers'?

Targs

Black gentle-maggot humps, spread long-grass to rimrock
once, rolled out their road, the first permanent-way
rails followed. Musk-ox before them, glacier's day,
terrace as cattle do, any slope that can stay
though there is nothing soft about their shield-under-forelock
and they shock roots of earth, shoots cropped and pulled up
Ontario and Appalachians and Bay over to Puyullyap
one huge hollow sounding board for hoofs, the continent;
the roar of their coming its mightiest wind.

Not roused by that tail flick lariat, starling-flocks
only recently alien, as they had been at the ancestors
and wisent, megaceros, the Eurasian aurochs
chaps' bear-berry stained, giving the game away
or have they been, like me. wallowing in Wallowa
like salmon of the Salmon ultimately Of No Return
bring me back to the offing, with such polite coughing
the quiet they had roused by their almost-silence
impetus mocking bear-hump; quantity commonsense

ablation after the glaciers had scoured, and loess
accumulation for the earth to be trodden, richest we guess
than any west of the best black chernozem steppes;
they bring back the climax of prairie going forward!

(Meeting Buffalo herd)

(Idaho, 1967)

Sami in their tipis ("Hilpes"?)
Finmark in the 'fifties
thick skin patched with thin skin
needle holes under flaps pantiled
almost a proggy, with the same skill
as waterproof as my 'ventile'
more windproof than the Grenfell

why is no skin scorched within?
the vent is canted with the wind
by adjusting it poles with the breath
of the outside, the fire on the inside
the whole/home a system like a tree
but one a nomad, northearth ride
and listening is the place to be

here he learnt, his descendants remind
what had been gathered wandering
eastward a hemisphere, time out of mind
coming hunter and with the seasons
the waters, iced over, or in the birch
a tipi can be made of like a canoe
every stitch reasons every resin glue.

George Catlin artist from the early 1830's

Miniaturist to Minotaur – portraitist
to/of The People and their Rights,
George Catlin their champion
painted dignity, last rites,
individual, land, and nation –
left fashionable Philadelphia
risked the arrow, received the pipe

gave up "the limited and slavish
arts in which I am wasting
life and substance for a bare living"
the salons and the galleries
for the real dignity of the prairie
people and to be their "historian"
risking life and art in his giving

his time will come as Important Artist
as he knew their times would not survive
or be cherished. "I have flown to their rescue …
… for they are doomed and must perish …
and the acquisitive world may hurl poison
and every besom of destruction
crush them to death … yet they may rise …"

Though he, too, painted only the essential
like my work, his has its 'stylised' hills
but not the flashiness of, say, Remington
and others – Bierstadt's – mountains
then so fashionably, lurid to exaggeration
not the idealism either of Fenimore Cooper
but a dignity that was real, naturalist.

England, even, encouraged him but an American
Joseph Harrison, architect of locomotion*
recognised the fellow craftsman in Catlin
rescued him from Debtors' Prison in London
at the price of unsold art and artefacts
(with Mammon, Catlin's only successful pact)

Six years on and beyond the frontier
on and beyond the Missouri, front-lines Rockies
"the world will surely be enough to forgive me
from this present unfinished and unstudied
art". The first real glimpse, before photography,
of The People in their Places, their last West
which, to them was North-South-East *and* West ...

Let pictograms, words and pictures show
Absaroka and Big Horn mountain-meadows
"buffaloes-range with the elk and the fleet
antelope; where the wolves are white
and bears grizzly; where the rivers are yellow"
cats all cougars "the dogs are all wolves"
hunters and warriors, their "men all lords".

Jackson Hole and Chicago, 1997

* builder of locomotives, Philadelphia

'Medicine Deer' Rock

come here to pray
the Plains Indian Way
and my own/your own way

climbing it better even
than Napes Needle
it is a gallery, no
it is an upthrust
of images of men
and of animals
(all one, then)
as in the caves, as out on the open fell

(Wake Forest is not) Wark Forest
as we go at it from Goat Farm

they impinge on each other less
than they overlie, palimpsest
generations of incised impressions
what generated them but that
but here the last
sundance before the
Custer Fight for
the Cheyenne some Lakota
and other of the Sioux
and Sitting Bull here had
his great vision (after
he had sacrificed of his own flesh)
of the grasshoppers falling into camp
as soldiers blue

Busby, Montana
1967, 1974

for John Busby and Dana Ivy (Wake Forest)

Equipment For Taxidermy

It was the beaver made the exploration
                                           the anthropologist
came along to skin out later
                                       begun before Rome and Greece
'Colt 45's only blew holes in them.'
                                     And Bowie knives
will open bone and tin, chop wood, do almost anythin'

'When we came here there must have bin beavers : 50 million
with the same blade we scalped all them'
                             Essential nature is in skin
PARKS' PERFUME. BASED ON CASTOREUM
                                               on a warm body!

Oregon 1973

Clark's Nutcracker
for Ronald H. Clark

      flatly   inexorably
      the box-canyons cracked-crate
is being forced by complex crazed extraverts   one or two birds but as if a whole rookery
berating   call them 'whiskey-jacks'
and not *Nucifraga caryocatactes*   but   *kraah krarr Nucifraga columbiana*
uncouth camprobbers crushing bores   churrr chatter characters, chatterboxes
foot-rattling cones to crash down the ripe ones   caricatures dont rate
waiting for, Idaho with a Dakotas head; feeling boxed-in and late.   Any state
their rockrough country manners make for early mornings, and hate-the-natives.

Colorado
1973

Ptarmigan

                    Night hardly begun   the spread lift sharp full to stun
                                              a blue star falls
– there is a gap among them there –   (there was)
                          – the moon is making the only other one –
a little smoke of snow up when its down
in days sharp white no sign of its softness
                                  the glare, the strain
but eye never near enough again.

Unalaska, in Montana winter 1975
for Martin McAsland

Great Northern Diver (her Common Loon) *for Lydia*

Long-call of loon
                    soon runs the length of the moon and back
far and dry and cool
                    but not, George Barker, 'as if it wished to die'
no bird, so much soul
                    in a song and out of it, going away and coining back
and ever will as we remember:
                          once heard, with the Killdeer and the Whippoorwill
the curlew on a springy hill,
              dismembered may be, whosever this is no cry, it fills
and carries back nights cracks the shooting star falling silverwhite and black
                        dissevers   forever   forever
and swings the lights still nearer the earth
death less than birth!

1979

loon-call for all long shorelines is horizon
neither repetition shortens nor stall it
neither do hill-line looms beyond extend it
where mudslide was loons echo is
sounds give avalanche by resonance

cambium between winter and spring rings
another annual growth, if you've time for both
winter long and spring late and a clean slate
where water and mist meet, rain and water
wind lulls wanting repeat, sweet dissonance

evident all distance went into this lake
one such slide would dam this river enough
carrying even trees gliding with their chickadees
as if nothing had happened, no event urgent
dalesmen and rangers have already forgotten it.

(landslips along Snake River, and the River Wear)
        both 1986

Snowy Owl, *for Laura*

Lift   nothing stealth
strength   nothing else
detachable   as if snow carded itself
                                    far fold to hold barred-bold
bird
dismissible deal below   white the world spins hardheard
shuffling cards coils diamonds dull white cools clubs spades coals real-slack glow
grow stars more starkly sparkle   eyes between us swivel slowly slow
presence here   farmfence   formless-force   as yet combs muskey beyond
pure shawl an owl; so across space out of it!
full of owl-right northern-lights van
catseyes at home on the road at night   blink

January 1976

MacKay's Snow-Bunting   *for Derek*

                              snowflakes   stay separate
                                    down stroke smoke stack-strew
            slow spiral blew
though fourteen inches deep   they have not buried seed-still-on-the-stem
the rush *Juncus squarrosus*   rakes   brakes   stays precipitate
the Buntings
        wait on the wired gate
                  as if for the others sake
                              as if its never too late or the day
will go on (but its winter-solstice's date)
                        each one's excited state   as if it drew
                ordered stake
     once or twice only rushes to the same snow crushes and picks up a few
only one *plucks* its seed; but there's no teamwork to shake them down as they could do
and clear the deck and not come back
                    shaking off others we
                              rate they co-operate with
                        :they leave some seed for you and me

Alaska '73, '75

Riding: The Platte, Nebraska

        it's as important to know the source of the river
only one can ever   be the giver
the rest are contributors
                      bearing
                     tributary

I hear the shuffling behind my mind
and find   only you   packing   parking smiles
for one to have integrity   bear the same name
through dilution
        through what seems chemically the same
but proven to taste different

                        deferent
            Platte
                      effluent
this is all I can be sure of   at the moment
the river is the same species of involvement

1976

Fire Place

Callahan   it was west of
Rifle   built his
Mantel   out of this outcrop
                sat back to listen to the hissin
on those first green loggins
                out of Pissin Creek*
and the whole house went up
                otherwise the place would have been forgotten
                Remembered for the Ute, the 'rock that burns
the oil-men out of Scotland, one of them
Calvinist   galvanised in sequence
recognised Cannel Coal
dug the trial hole
assayed   'a single square mile of Piceau
would yield a million barrels of shale-oil,
100,000,000 tons of soda-ash
                forty million tons of alumina.'

Colorado / Wyoming

*The modified name 'pee-ants'

Padding Words Stalk Some Passing Cat

As the record droned on, I realised
that the voice was E.E.Cummings'
for all that there were capitals: each word its own cloud of knowing
needing no visual punctuation, nuclear, predicating diction
of its own patterned patter, mannered matter.
Not so much needing space around it as using it well
happening enough to me to set down figurine, leviathan
to caravans coming, camels padding soft over Indian dunes
that pouring of grit, or the hoppers continual to the Furnaces
of Gary, that harrier *Circus cyaneus* hanging on the wind for Harry
laughing of air interfaces in spaces between feathered fingers,
April as this is not the cruellest month
in Europe: in America everything ...
everyone else realises the record is still running on.

Mount Rainier

Avalanching, earthing thunder, bird
message-print of wing-brush snow
twist-tumult of dry torrent, Kautz Creek
split timber, every echo 'go'.

Us, the last of your winter, Mount Rainier
remembering to stress the last syllable
like primary-feathers flexing on downstroke
like life returning, and capable. So.

My mud packed in your quiet volcano
its head blown off, waiting for the word
written. Nothing to tell mudruns from thunder
or some avalanche of snow. We heard

the whine of waggons only, the tamp of trucks.

1973

Aplomado Falcon

motion so near the earth its own slow lure
cresting a col the road used quick
east into Texas on a southwest wind
winnowing fairhead falcon finned
(Yorkshire merlin beat against the northeaster at Scarth Nick
notch in the hills and gateway to the moor)

trod unexpected air, feathered
stalled to sheltered sagebrush

gone-away before more than naming could be sure
is most experience though
slowing almost to a stall is not the way we expect at all
but to see the pattern,
not only at altitude spins the hub
this plateau makes its own bird-herding net
eyes own ideas

Edwards Plateau 1973, 1977

from Black Hambledon – Black Hills Songs

(Black Hambledon)

moon rising on   and sun
                            lost one   world   young
croppin all now   land won
                                sung   mystic-mountains rung
different drum and different song
north   outcrops blacken rimrockfaces
south rimrock faces shake aspen asking
                                   describe a circle
lighten and dance with mineral traces
                                earth shakes
changed songs would never change it
                                around bills
where pines arent so high now spring is drying?
badlands-nearer   to their own earth-mother.

Creation is going-on   each feather   each morning
becomes a new eagle   so it is to the man
who doesnt know the story   but has the eagle-feather
and looks at it each morning
                              doesnt show it to every-one.

(Sturgis)

what he does see is   the horizon, and below
that dead thing between his fingers isnt one-of-them
cigarette old-and-oily mechanic iris-in-the-eye gone stark
some pain strays over stays

                                  tourists Rushmore Rednecks shore
                         we are as afraid of Indians as of Gypsies
                berry-brown-round-Indian-head selling bunches of heather
                   in parallel evolution asked me, in the market, for a pencil

      and when offered a pen the light died in her eyes, used as screwdriver
          what the derelicts tell tall isnt necessarily unruly unreliable
                                                                 at all while
the eyes dont lie   or the stall in speech   or the shift of the feet at the wall
                                                            life tenses
            Do not fear the snake   let him come to you
          if you are hungry and you ask him he can replace even buffalo

                                ... the snake catches up during the night
        and stays with you for the winter   even if you kill him.

(by Harley-Davidson, 1976:
some years later the company
named a model for Sturgis)

(Topcliffe, Up the Escarpment)

                                                              and the Lokrian-Sikelian
                                                                        Peace Treaty
                  The 1968 Caravan Act as "honoured" as the 1868 Fort Laramie Treaty:
                                                                        we never should
play with the gypsies in the wood   distinct men in England?
                                    even Geordies are Giorgified:
                          where are your tribes gone, we men have tried
                       we Romani, Didicoi, Yenish, Sinti, all Travellers
                              we keep some spirit and some morals,
             houses less healthy than horses, stealing children, over-drinking!
Life dances in through inertia, because of things, round, even square dancing
   the art of asking-very-little but ever in or of the world, horses slowly prancing
           the schoolhouse stars-and-stripes dust-gathering, North Riding children
                                                           bussed to town:

fire must be carried in the hand: if you look at Chinese, or us, understand
it is here where we are now   not there that we all share the same face
what we all choose   where the problem starts and the land begins to lose;
the gods are not exclusive   Muskrat   Beaver   Watergod   Kingfisher
Morningstar Flying Squirrel Great Bear Snake Wolf
Turtle Fox Not Exclusive Man

(Bad River, Teton, For A.W.)

titon wan; dwellers-in-the-prairies ... oglala; scattering our own
Paha Sapa centre where the earth is medicine-mother Makar; Makapeezu t'wing
turnip and crane little-spirits-who-carry-news (late-sixties Chevrolet Impalas)
the watchers-in-the-sky are on-their-way to 'the' gods to be in love with turnip, crane
arrow-fletch from moulted waterfowl and with the Greeks the Athene Pallas owl
so small it can go anywhere: east is light, west in not in strife with him. (Kyote or Speotyto)
totem we all have the authority and the responsibility, the world is as tree, not linearly
from a cave base we came out, all of us, these hills are so in all of us
Black Hills for all of us The People
Human Beings
seeing.

for Renville, Santee Sioux

We wanted to look at War Cloud's paintings, like hanging about
outside the little Telford's Library at Langholm for the shout from the rivers
that sent you out, Chris Grieve, on your career of leading out
by words like migrant birds over oceans. As I have remembered you will remember
that rabbit on the steps of the Pohlen Art Center in Sisseton
where Renville stood a while to talk to use eyes beyond both of us
a warmth and gentleness and slight mustiness hopped around all of us.
His hopes on a new job, Benet pleased at that, me flitting at that rabbit
not focussing on it, on Renville or on Benet
                                                        but on the cut-off slopes beyond
the slipp-off of the Missouri Coteau   shown shorn by the too late sun
told Renville I'd ride back to Mankato where, to date, I have started a poem, sung
about that chief dead of a cannonball   where thirty-eight of his relatives had been hung
which without Lincoln had been three hundred and three
and when I came back, he'd talk, take to me.

Mankato, Minn. Oct. 75
Langholm, Scotland Oct. 76

Short Stack With Navaho

The controlled wobbling way
a skeleton walks
Eliot carried all his books to the attic
against the time
his rookery's contrivance strained against the silence

we may have displaced bones
bending under loads
inherited ossifications out of the north
softness out of the south
but one to another talks against the raven of wreck.

St. Louis 1973

Bobcat

                    like-lynx
not recognised at first   then
(as the puma is the friend of man)
dark pace raking lands   hands switch
     a weaving tail-light [it
putting the feet down broad   as playing
too lightly lines   leaving after so little
notes struck, so softly
        feeling the little air linger
     the brittle finger shaking hands and heads. after
doubt (eyes that   stay   bright)   of identity
                (fit)

Cascade Range 1979

NNWP

        What he would have found, on either hand …
        from Desolation Sound to mid-Vancouver Island
Ish River Sound's body in Puget Sound; its wings the straits of Juan de Fuca
and the great Fraser River… between the Olympics and the Cascades crests and Coast ranges …
        Ish River is a great bowl of green waters.
        The chart of rivers in its southern half
        includes (clockwise from S.E. to N.W.:
        Hamma-hamma, Duckabush, Doseywallip.
        Kwil Kene, Grey Wolf, Dungeon-ness,
        Elwha, Hoko. Pysht
        Sekiv, Fraser, Nooksack,
        Samish, Skagit, Stillaguamish.
        Snohomish, Skykomish. Snokwalnice.
        Duwarmish, Puyallup, Niskwally,
        Deschutes, the Sound, Skokomish.

Cascadia: *Planet Drum Review*, 1986

Beaver-Lodge reality; a Sioux who had *been in* Mene-sela.
His wisdom treated as nonsense by Parkman*, who set seal
on American, European ideas of reality as to the Indian ideas
for centuries. He didn't see 'legends', 'traditions', 'notions' of the Indians
as possibly any kind of reality. These themselves are real powers.
His wisdom insight, consensus of the village, tribe, whole civilisation
for all it may have seemed no more than leaves, transient as flowers.

Mene-sela's vision because he had endured the journeying-in
"to see what was there", in and through the "dark, cold, and close" state
so that he was losing 'normal' consciousness, "almost suffocated"
sometimes had to swim to see, realise in the emptiness the meaning
of The People seals, beavers, bears, 'human-beings' beginning
an enlightenment in science and in art, a whole work no more rated
of value than any we patronise as 'childish imaging, imagining'

[e.g. in *The Oregon Trail* 1849: His brief experience had been in the summer of 1846]

Being in the Bin
or the Irrelevance of 'Recycling'
for Roy Fisher, his Furnace

The beauty and intensity of stripping
off scrapyard and its universal tipping
into the furnace our future and present
all a city is, all we writers can represent

Whitman asked in Leaves of Grass
"The friendly and flowing savage.
Is he waiting for civilisation
or past it and mastering it?"
You do not get the answer to this
 in Whitman, or on the Reservation:
"… red life flows in a different direction"

under the light over the mountains
and inside the light by prairie rivers
is to be on a range of wavelengths
overlapping the taiga's, and the ocean's
and the ice's – especially *its* strengths
and the high desert southwestwards
bare as thighs presents and represents
elements of all that 'civilisation'
that continuity original – American
Navaho no less than Zuñi show
no more than Sioux or Esquimaux …

Thoreau's Penobscot guide to Woodland
provokes questions; he has no answer:
"one revelation has been made to the Indian,
another to the white man". We infer
we are no further on, need to be in.

Yes, yet a requirement for the poet
as for the Indian is not to answer the question
[Hemingway and Eliot helped
clean out the language –

the Anglo-American lingo
which, we say, is not at all *American* ...]
nor even to tell it, for the narrative
is everything, its own truth, and *English*
is as poor at telling anything 'native'.

After being with the people of the salmon
to the river Salmon and on to Ketchum
beads of water jumped from the line
that tightened beyond the taut
as the marlin pulled, the boat
began to move, and his sentence
umiak after the pilot-whale fine
black line bobbing its skin float
its giving-itself; no dive, its defence

It is all another way around
once we have watched the smell and sound
winding the scene, nor needed hallucinogen
once we have watched hawk over and again
at work, pondered his relation and origin

'Reality' is relative or we'd not need Einstein.
It was an English bookstore manager's question
(a statement really) that my poems were fiction.
In a strange land, Heinlein, we don't expect the stranger
and I was glad in a little way to be a danger
so that they were not reviewed in his newspaper
(to which I was a regular contributor!)

High Rockies. October 1997

Sprightly they go in casuistry
(argument set-aside one more day)
Montana into Wyoming dreams
Idaho also, teem before the snow
gleams, indifferent of identity
dull days full of haze and grays.
Coyote lean a-slope seeming
slim as stoat, droll as tall troll
strolls fall-in-willow-shadow pebble-
shoal half-wolf without his bulk
sulky doggedness or sullen lope;
or doubled-up fox, as sharp a nose,
hope-fear steers route scent disposes:
Elk already down and belling, show.

Moose move marsh alongside its floor
widening for fall-roar yet to come, before;
cottonwoods' awning. barriers to its own corridor
river delivers their road, grown-hollow-way
parallels buffalo-road, beaver-detailed course;
sunk so their great hulk little shows, subsides,
and what does glows green algal blooms hides…
Coyote gleans deermice, meadow vole, crisp
their woodrush fruits, gramma-seeds. Reeds whisper
where deer has been, tell bear, bend scent
meant more than transmitted, as with us:
doves also give game away. Tropes go away;
we are too slow to know, yes, as yet
aspects of sense we have only just met.

'American Marten, Replacing the Pine Marten In England'
       (at the gamekeeper's vermin-line)

The ending of leaf-year.
      Squirrel-cats, as red as Indian, as dead
        a hundred years after we cleared them off our land
   a panic of birds brought them back.
Slipping from fur farms, trapped origins in America,
                 to live feral in Northumberland
   break silhouettes, slim Sitka spruce
   mark mathematical moods of forest
   penetrative of pile Lodgepole pine
   print marten visiting-cards, violet scats.
      Inquisitive of woodmen and willed walkers.
Scents in stir.

1972

'G.T.T. 1884'

(inscription on the headstone of a New Englander,
Gone to Texas) for J. K., Houston.

To where there are no stratus-clouds,
no wandering in raw air for radicals.
For breathing-spaces, knowing very deep
blur with me the edge of desert's heat
as I cannot speak my dialect to you
starting your rhythms straight from the heart
in England from the heartland of America.
                    They open Auden

The desert is exfoliating stones, as ripples,
and opening Auden was not the thing to do:
Auden born in York but not yet brought to stand,
sending nucleated abstractions to hot presses.
Your images, southern and not sudden, swell
words out of a well, artesian, out of depth
is your music of stars and stones and sand?
                    They listen to the stones

Here in old York, dialecting raw again,
trying to contract these stones to flowering.
Scrolled on paper; your vowels roll droll
as if you said them with a rounded chisel
clean on red outcrops where the sun is towering,
to show pronouncements to every passing modern
and you will teach my ear to read music.
                    They see, and hear.

1971

Pieces from 'Climbing'   (Book 5 of For 'Tea at Forty')

                                                          Waking, drunk, the Black Hills above Sturgis
    some rime of Wyoming still lime sticky thistle bourboned playing about the lips
      slaking some species of thirst off the stones sipping mountain stripped split pine
        urge is its own shadow of actions climbing riding dreaming all time

                                                we go
                                   higher but not cooler
              the stones smoother and hotter   no shade and their sun nearer
and no movement of air as there had been in the pines below, no movement and no shadow
only the question soberer and soberer why we go
and wait language languid so
enough to be of the stones, peeling under sun and snow alike not pliant as pines in their own
wavelength of wind   but skinned rawhide   all else beside fitting its own answer.

The Black Hills. S.D./Wyo.

Hell Canyon, On Snake River, Idaho 1973

Naked in staked air-envelope taking inverted massif of Snake
   embraced seams roaring down sounds rocking 5,000' face
      pent streams fur, gold, water-power-to-be firmament
        the original RIVER OF NO RETURN for Lewis and Clarke
          killing skills kill conscience sunslit scorching
            scored soft-shoe narcissism scorned
              scissored hurts Nez Percé bursts
              sharp rock the land shock hurts!
                sockets burn skinstark
                  forest skirts up irk
                    come bland go
                      stand follow
                        swallow
                          swirl
                          dark
                           eye

The Pine Ridge Gyrfalcon

Look he is in river in the air/heaven over the dry land, the stale Bad
contrast his silver presence in the weak sunlight with contrail
he is of the second and gone on it faster than that jetplane
miles under the jetstream   or only seems
Falcon   arrow with long tangs
  as if relics of some storm the breughs in the clouds
  prism even after he's passed through, like his claws
  shreds of cloud he has cut himself, ribbon, shrouds
rang the changes of bell-peals by his shuffle of syllables
consonants of fuselage, clipped consonants of wingbeats' primaries
unheard harmonies of axillaries and mantle-feathers arrowed
with vees backward, the only marks he carries thus, for speed
as for distinction of rank   grey-blue seam of slate
or whin   but really of a soft metal: gleams ice like the gley
                    sliced by the spade after a death

like after my first real English gyr (a Westmorland) he said "reek, man, reck"

how she, an elegant, spoke out for her place and people
to the visiting bird 'seen oh we brought'. Gladys Bissonette

                          (not not a 'little Buffalo')

One bird is a flock in itself
(Schoolchild, Pine Ridge)

          birds bring own news from God
          standing on the glacier when the brokken
          shadow (of self) rears up with the sun
          as from behind that cloud, as from
          a gun, as from behind is the bird
          screeched silent over the rusticol
          under us; drying glacier of the arid
          aqueducted a word and the bird
          shower of faint sleet on the wind

Prairie

A prairie place to the strains of Rock of Ages and a High Plains Wind

We are all related
                        and the hills are ringed round again by singing artillery
this is our strength our people
                        the church pockmarked headhigh, sweat-tent rock-steady
the idea of religion is foreign for us
                        the saved buffalo-robe was imported.

                       000

Prairie Gentian calms Wolf and 31st Street, fifteen miles West of the Loop
gentle Closed Gentian by train-rails, sages, wild rose
Gentiana puberla Gentiana andrewsii
Artemisia, Rosa Carolina
seven-foot Blue Stem Grass
cracking 'twenties concrete
where there would have been eighty city blocks
                                     wounding needing
                                                 churches.

Pine Ridge, South Dakota – Illinois; Wolf Road

The Book of Nature

Red pine's the new bulkhead for my books
baulks by Baltic, or corded in America
bulk to condensing annual strata
in journals remembering dust is years' dismember,
but resining new cleats with celtic thongs
reddening through lusty singing the old songs.
Time's erosion to tone-leading weathered looks
as redgrit fretted, current-bedded, your
sediment grown landscape, level headed
insisting diction on what? Viking
aboriginal, Northumbrian, grown
singsong guttural, Red Indian
the book of the life, new-biggin,
stone grown grain cut cross-rhythms.

original version 1:3:71
(for his 71st birthday)

New Airframe   *for C. Furr, Utah*

Stalling a Texan's "biggest" story, these remains are –
      'too big to take-off, how-so-ever.'
Old bones we make
      leak creek in dry weather
                skin stretch minds?
                        Never!
    : 'Not on 25-foot thin membranes'
                    so not on your
capacity
    beyond aerodynamic theory but on
category they voted.
        On a relative calm, even
                    my 500-three
Kawasaki practically floated, gas-mileage improved
                we were with the dust
    clinging loose to the land as it passed under us
near to flying and without really trying.
      In Great Basins then, over Great Plains
    then as now there'd be mainly wind, rare rains
the furry fifty-foot span could lift   and soar:
not reptile nor bird nor mammal
              Pterosaur

Big-Bend / Edward's Plateau
Texas, April 1973

from Tea at 40

a locomotive trundling west over dry sticks
                                       North Yorkshires sand devils –
are planing across the road with bits of their hedges in them and the high tension
coming off one at a time   the motor to stutter before full song again
at   (kph) 140   the throttle-grip position irrelevant   and drying skin
afterwards   words leaning forward walking   how lovely the fresh land after
paradoxically every scent as if enclosed in hedges   my doxie still between knees
                       after the big, long wind
     Crossed arms of field, the shadows merge for the night
   the light side of the brush lines holding bright as birch as if the sun was white
   the dark dusts tryst wring out mists breath between shallow wreath – fallows bust
   at its going-down to renewal neither eye admits to rust
   woolpile packs full mile sachs close to the heave to follow furrow hoam
   loose pylons ask cloud which is way, the witches' broom its nests and distance foam
   in our slowing down to refuel guts dont reduce. Lost loam.

   some song his cane from wind, unpinned
   The Pacific Northwest Power Company has already marked their tones
   High Mountain Sheep Dam, Low Mount Sheep Dam, Appaloosa Dam   and
   Pleasant Valley Dam;   which will beggar the wild turbulent Snake, bones
   polished ribs, plates overlapping ventrally, polished scales and pot-holes
   ferns shaking narrows, willow brakes all the way down to Hells Canyon Dam
   they are going to name this construction cynically after the Nez Percé
   whose survivors scramble for a living down there in Seattle, Oregon, Spokane,
   the Nez Percé whose thief Joseph had used this ravine to avoid the military
   his careful barefoot breakout for freedom foxing through Seven Devils, Imnaha Defiles
   in 1877 until over the Salmon and just thirty bare miles short of the Canada border
   — where there was thin ice cover there were shallow kettles after :
   man now no less effective hand on the land than that longlost glaciation
   This will be the last big dam, said the man with the Power Boat
          the west is not only Power Reclamation
   dare I say exploitation   we look to such as Senator Church and Parkman
   to promote a National River area for such canyon-conservation

               the mist comes up with the adders out of the ground
                 just before the sun because of the day and the night before

     Washington Irvings   rising like gigantic walls and battlements

                                      Hell's Canyon on the Snake, Oregon/Idaho 1973

Quake, Communicate

Thin skin bland white black eyed
            lining shallows lightening shadows
                                      swinging setting sun
                September through April deepening cutover where
      we all exhibit con-tent toward the winter.
Winds most blatantly stripped tree   violently
                            repeats the mountain states in their own waters;
              show us your relating to the birch
rubbing.our.way.out.of.velvet wapiti enlivened by your movement, our Red Deer.

Spread yellow-furred stain, stiff soil
                        never super-saturate, stir, always foil fuller
bark just the pink side of white as of sun flashes black show when, buff,
its Clark's Nutcracker shows up where he can least be noticed, or fear colors,
everything heard the bird the tree to each other speak wing swing silently
                marsh march gully shrilly stammer
                    fen shimmery
          quake-aspen   after summer.

Colorado 1973

The Cypress Hills and Barrens

appear   Snow buntings in snow
up here   always a flock of similar size in such weather
snow-buntings land and take-off in a scatter but together
no system   though there is some sudden same-pattern
each bird its part   its own part but not the same part always, or its neighbour
line-foraging ahead
                spinning tension in watcher
                                        maintaining strain on the skein –
to the snapping-point where they all each   take   off   again.
and I get a fresh line on a lie of a land

land without standing, blow but more slowly   strow some hollows   their loose-flurry
aerial scurry   snowflakes random the   wake of line squall   fencepost   woodedge
and most, the break of slope of the hill of the poor heaves of the muskeg
            cleaves jack pine stands and seaves where the snow has sifted thinnest
quick over the surface   tuft to tuft   just   a run here   a little punt ahead there
the congregation for seeds downwind of the place the wind keeps bare where is it?
excitement that same instability   that seeds finding ability
this is   where it is to find   mind same, despite appearance; poet.

Canada 1975

Agelaius phoeniceus

"Strength of will keeps me here"
Same wind over the tule *Scirpus* stems tu-*lee*
steady pedestrian   persistently reedy
shares songs with other blackbirds but distinctive, almost diagnostic okee -*lee* pkie -*ree*
the pitch rising on the final syllable:
over the prairie Provinces, through the States' great plains; in almost every slough,
the Red-winged Blackbird seems   is heard before it is *seen*

thick-billed over the grasslands, thinner billed elsewhere   and why
arid and its seeds, insects, chards are harder there. "Forget provincial frontiers!"

Mississippi Floods at Moline, April 1973

'Forty three feet over and still rising'
more than any parting of a country's air
emotion from the Shield right through to the Bayoux
        mud-stirrer muck spreading from Saskatchewan
        shit sharer, share crop destroyer biggest known
        in history all of a hundred years or two.
Remembered what the Ark's pigeon brought back to Noah
the farmer from Olive Branch told how Cons from Vienna
the Pen will shovel to save Cairo in Illinois,
        An ye hev tishoot thim grund hogs
        the floodwater'll git in their holes in these levees
        fur the river to *blow*. Levy Army Engineers,
Incontinent, divider, inconsequent provider silt
pans out fresh razmataz around New Orleans
muskrat rambling delta discharge fertiliser.

Smelt

What you were saying about mass media
coloring images and colonising minds
I take develop other senses then.
                                        Water
the perfect solution   we are in
needs no tide to wash   its rich smelt out of Michigan
our imagination   is that they breed inshore
in fact   the creeks are too damned for them
they die   intestate ovate or big testes.
        Nature will not be understood with
        but understated while even the salt in the blood
        is overestimated for someone or other's end
        we're too material in this sense even in
        the Conservation Chapter in South Bend,
on each tide   shadows
once ripples lived in each wave's phrasing   stipples
we learn to write before we read   on shore
what does not matter any more.

Michigan

The Place You Recommend

That record snow of April is in me
nervousness about the thing I love
hesitates me at the edge
as if its clouds had to fill my valley
mesa my little stacks of information
with your love on edge.

My strata, level, cut to pediments
high-angle sides, support a little growth
of scrub. Fourteen miles
to the other side. I hesitate, you wait
as if the spirit knew we worshipped him
and not here, your smiles.

This, the place you recommended
but you did not come yourself.
Rockshelf cuts out its stars. extended.
                              Untended
the years before meeting
unending.

1973-2003

New Drift Country   post-Impressionists: the colours
its texture   a whitish-brown to the grass
sharp-shadowed terracettes where the dairy-cattle pass
tack little red-brown sails
                republican country looks right with stands of pine
in shelterbelts and steeps
cut out mask for smiling theatres cutovers lie and alders line
between moraines and eskers   syllables
levelled for lumber   drain corn to the dilute eye

Wisconsin 1975

'Passenger Pigeon, Extinct 1914'

      (at the birdskin cabinet)

'Warming days
 can bring no more from the south.'
                                     Fan of a continent
your wings are stiff to flight
   like so much nineteen-fourteen extinct.
Each year this skin scales tighter to the reptile
                             Archaeopteryx launched
to fall in heaps to guns
 where arrows and falcons
            once had singled out forever.
And the same sun searches clearings for nothing now
and scorching, even in April.
                    Arrowheads to blacken the skies of America
have passed into the void extinction is
 where there are not even clouds to darken.

1964

Mass-Movement

Everyone alone
            in each territory you see
the land split here 14 miles, millions of years deep
so that the animals along the South Ridge
have never seen their neighbours on the North Ridge
for thousands of generations.

A shadow brings no rain to State and Michigan Avenue,
cliff-dwelling crags of new baboons on their hadramaut
listened to the vibrations of the pueblo, built same sandstone
caves some state of mind, stepping-stones of poured declivity
still desert kinds of habitation;
arid of air-conditioning, not graduated of Grand Bedu.

Arizona and Chicago

From an Unfinished 'American' Long-Poem

After a few days birding on the desert plateaus
the main street ablaze at noon in Amarillo
and soaring in that inner mirage Basil, your visage
advertising your *Collected Poems* all a bookshop window
soaring somehow with its presence, as a hawk is.
The day is fatal, the preaching is of The End
(revivalistically)
and you realise, after a while, these people believe it, are in some way ready for these Last Days
(and realistically)
taken for granted more than a concentration camp for people would be; it is more clinical
three hundred miles from the next city, frontier town where anything might go:
the pure (in faith) will subscribe and survive The Lake of Fire, the Inferno!
There had been talk of Pantex, as if of the local ladies underwear manufactory
(that may have saved men, for these days, from the Dustbowl
some of them OKies, most of them bible belters), or
an Exhibition Centre to outdo all others such,
a place there'd be a hypermarket at, and sports.
It is for All, but all the nuclear weapons of these United States, their Final Assembly.
Bible literally true, so one day Up We All Will Go. It pays most of the wages and to charities.
The desert would take the place over again without Pantex, and the necessity for a Pantex is
pantechnical for Tribulation. Tribes impervious to the presence of the panacea Pantex
out on the desert the scarps that roll about Amarillo are only waves of
the day stifled stiff succulents bend a little on the evening breeze
audibly and far from the road they are the only noise
before the scuttling evening-lizards
both plants and lizards open their pores
automatically, we'd say
after the fatal day
the one to fix carbon, from the carbon dioxide released by even the desert's life
the other to breathe the oxygen, release the dioxide, let the quiver run along the spine
and find the stunned-by-the-sun's-fusion legions of windblown insects from the leafy suburbs
pick off his quota of live nocturnal invertebrates, (sap) still wet within not needing to drink
    otherwise
so many of the inhabitants sedated and secured by the system within they're even not needing
    to drink otherwise
and never look at the desert save through glass; never feel the desert save through rubber, are
    saved from any of that.

[These 34 lines from the draft of an 'American' long-poem for him were sent from West Texas early in 1976 when Bunting was himself on a reading tour in the United States. He replied from New England commenting on an 'improvement' on an earlier draft and looking forward to some further "post-mortem dissections" if he "ever got back from this mad whirligig".]

www.ingramcontent.com/pod-product-compliance
Lightning Source LLC
Chambersburg PA
CBHW082120230426
43671CB00015B/2751